D1060810

JEWISH SOCIAL STUDIES MONOGRAPH SERIES
NUMBER 1

THE GHOSTS OF 1492

Jewish Aspects of the
Struggle for Religious Freedom in Spain
1848–1976

CAESAR C. ARONSFELD

NEW YORK 1979

DISTRIBUTED BY COLUMBIA UNIVERSITY PRESS

DS135
S7
A76

© Copyright 1978
Conference on Jewish Social Studies

Library of Congress Catalogue Card No.
78-71448

ISBN 0-910430-00-4

Printed in the United States of America by
Capital City Press, Inc.

CONTENTS

MAR 27 1980

Grateful acknowledgement is made of the kind and generous assistance received from: the Librarian of the London Hispanic Council, Mr. George Green, and his (then) assistant, Señorita Susana Medina; the Librarian of the Mocatta Library (London University College), Mr. Roy C. Fincken, and the archivist, Ms. Gertrude Levy; and from the Librarian of Jews' College, London.

FOREWORD

The Board of Directors of the Conference on Jewish Social Studies and the Editors of its Journal are happy to announce the start of a new Monograph Series. For a long time the need has been felt for an outlet to publish worthwhile studies covering limited areas in the Jewish social sciences which are too large to be included in our Journal and, yet, too small to appear in book-length volumes. We believe that Monographs ranging from fifty to one hundred printed pages (some 25,000 to 50,000 words) would answer that need. It is only now with the financial assistance of Jewish Cultural Appeal of the National Foundation for Jewish Culture that we are able to bring this long anticipated series to fruition.

It gives us great pleasure to open the new venture with *THE GHOSTS OF 1492: Jewish Aspects of the Struggle for Religious Freedom in Spain 1848–1976* by Caesar C. Aronsfeld. This volume concerns itself with little-known aspects of the Jewish struggle for civil liberties and religious freedom during the last century and a half. It is a remarkable episode in the long struggle for Jewish Emancipation. Unlike most other countries, Spain was debating not only the merits of what rights were to be extended to the Jews, but the very question of readmitting them to the country and establishing Jewish communities enjoying complete religious freedom. These matters had long been decided in the affirmative in most western countries even before the Emancipation era.

In this struggle the relatively few Jews who had already been living in Spain played a minor role. It was left to some interested Jewish leaders of other lands as well as to a number of Spanish liberal statesmen and publicists to propose the return of the descendants of the former exiles and the admission of other Jews under conditions of freedom. Time and again, however, their efforts encountered strong resistance from conservative and ecclesiastical circles still dominated by "The Ghosts of 1492" and the racialist tradition of *limpieza*.

The story of these debates and occasional negotiations is dramatically told in this small volume. It is an object lesson demonstrating that medieval intolerance still remains a living tradition in a civilized, modern nation.

Mr. Aronsfeld is a member of the Institute of Jewish Affairs in London, editor of the bimonthlies, *Patterns of Prejudice* and *Christian Attitudes on Jews and Judaism*, and the author of numerous essays on contemporary and historical aspects of Jewish life. He also contributed to our Journal. Mr. Aronsfeld enjoys a fine reputation as a thoughtful and thought-provoking essayist.

Conference on Jewish Social Studies
Jeannette M. Baron
President

THE GHOSTS OF 1492

Jewish Aspects of the Struggle for Religious Freedom in Spain

Spain is a somber figure in Jewish history, a memorial to the fickleness of man's fortunes that will rise to the stars and fall to wretched depths. Such was Spain's own fate and such was the fate of her Jews who first enjoyed a "Golden Age" and then, ironically in the year of the discovery of America, were cast adrift, degraded and despised, into an exile that never seemed to end. Other countries too banished their Jews — England in 1290 and France in 1391 — yet there always was a return, and the dates of the expulsion were hardly remembered. The year 1492, however, stands out in Jewish minds: a landmark to be compared only to the destruction of Jerusalem in 70 or the advent of Hitler in 1933; and through the centuries it has barred any thought of a large-scale return. Spain and the quixotic cause of her "Catholic unity" have been apt to arouse among Jews the emotions of classical tragedy, terror and pity. Jews never settled in Spain again in anything near their previous numbers, and even now they are woefully few — some 12,000 in a total population of 35 million.

It may seem strange that there should be so few, and occasionally in fact it is believed that, while a fair number returned to England and France once permitted to do so, Jews steadfastly refused to go back to Spain, having solemnly excommunicated the cruel land. The truth is that no such *Herem* was ever pronounced — neither on Spain nor on any of the countries that drove out their Jews.[1] Actually Spain never was cleared of Jews by the Catholic sovereigns, Ferdinand and Isabella, when they issued the fateful Banishment decree of 31 March 1492; crypto-Jews were probably as frequent there as in Elizabethan England, and for centuries Spain was beset by what became known as the black and white Judaism — "the observance of the law of Moses in preference to the precepts of the Church" and "the white Judaism which includes all kinds of heresy such as Lutheranism, freemasonry and the like."[2]

The memory of the Jews — and their usefulness — never vanished from Spain. Toward the end of the seventeenth century, the prime minister of Charles II, Manuel de Liras, hoped to relieve the nation's economic distress by bringing the Jews back. "Well intentioned and zealous for the public good . . . he did not hesitate to draw the Supreme Council's attention to the expelled

1

Hebrew race. . . . Well aware of the strong opposition he was bound to meet by as much as mentioning them, he nevertheless named the Edict of 1492 as the only obstacle to a mitigation of the troubles from which they all suffered."[3] He cited the example of Holland which was enjoying prosperity owing to this "discreet policy." Nothing came of the project, though the idea was not forgotten. About a hundred years later, in 1786, a Royal Order, dated 25 April, actually permitted the entry of Jews who had a license from the king.[4] In 1797, it was revived by the then Minister of Industry and Trade, Pedro de Varela, who recommended to Charles IV "the admittance of the Hebrew nation to Spain,"[5] because "general opinion agrees [he wrote in a memorandum dated 21 March] that they own the largest amount of wealth in Europe," and so this project "would serve to balance the affairs of state by increasing the commerce and industry in a way which no other measure will ever effect." He suggested that the government enter into negotiations with "some of the principal Jewish houses in Holland [and] of the free cities of northern Europe," with a view to establishing suitable factories in Cadiz and other Spanish ports. Once this was done, "the country might then be thrown open to the whole of the Hebrew nation" who, Varela added, had "never forgotten the advantages and amenities they once enjoyed in Spain."[6]

What he had in mind was a royal decree as radical as that of 1492. Of course, if only because of the Inquisition still in force, it did not have a chance, and the government rejected the idea as "risky to the point of adventurous and contrary to the laws of the land." In fact, shortly after, on 27 May 1802, all laws and regulations relating to the treatment of Jewish would-be immigrants were explicitly upheld by a royal decree ordering the rigorous execution of all the penalties provided. This decree was reaffirmed on 16 August 1816 after the Napoleonic wars had offered a good many opportunities which Jewish enterprise was not likely to miss. The tribunals of the Inquisition became perplexed by the influx of Jews at Algeciras, Cadiz and Seville, but although strict enforcement of the previous orders was demanded, the secular officials now seemed slow to cooperate. The inspection of ships, for example, was no longer carried out with any severity, and some ports revealed that, as a result, increasing numbers of Jews were arriving.[8]

Exit the Holy Inquisition

These Jews were still Marranos. There were "certain holy families" who enjoyed "much consideration" among their brethren,[9] and these, for the most part were traders from North Africa or Gibraltar. They lived in the hope that the days of the Inquisition were numbered; this strong arm of the medieval Church had been variously abolished in Spain (22 February 1813) and restored (21 July 1814),[10] until it was outlawed for good by the Royal Decree of 15 July

1834,[11] though its ghost kept stalking about the land for some time yet. Religious freedom was still far from its dawn. Some governments were not unwilling to move forward, notably that of the Marrano Prime Minister Mendizábal, "the wandering Jew come back to politics,"[12] but the Church was powerful enough to stifle the effort. The Bible was taboo, unwanted as a "Jewish book."[13]

The idea of tolerance, however, was in the air. Spaniards began to see "the great error and injustice" of the expulsion.[14] In 1847 the learned Adolfo de Castro who had already written a "History of the Persecution of the Protestants by Philip II," published a "History of the Jews in Spain," wherein he declared: "The Catholic Sovereigns, in ordering the banishment of the Jews, acted in direct opposition to the rules of justice and the honour of the Gospel, and instead of rendering a real service to the Spanish nation, did it infinite mischief, the effects of which we feel even to this day."[15]

Castro deemed it politic to mention that he was "neither a Jew nor a descendant of Judaizers," but he felt it was time to tell the truth that had been "corrupted by historians." He said, "What praises have they not lavished upon the catholic zeal of Ferdinand the Fifth for exterminating the Jews," as if it had been proof of "Christian piety." He was not "going to palm off covetousness and robberies as Christian acts." He was sure he would incur "the ill-will of many who will be silly enough to accuse me of being a bad Spaniard, merely because I do not allow my pen to repeat the errors which, up to this time, have falsified the history of my country. But I would ask those who would brand me with the imputation of being a bad Spaniard for speaking ill of bad Spaniards —is not the unhappy Jewish race which, through its misfortunes, has been domiciled in these lands ever since the seventieth year of the Christian era, as Spanish as our own?" The book was translated into English in 1851 by a Cambridge Protestant clergyman who, in an introduction, called upon the Spanish Queen Isabella "to make reparation to the Jews for the wrongs done to their race by her ancestors, and especially by her namesake: let her blot out from the statute-books of Spain every penal law that affects the Israelites; let her invite them back to the land which they still regard as the land of their adoption."[16]

Whereas Castro was eminently enlightened, another, writing almost simultaneously though independently, José Amador de los Rios, was curiously ambivalent. He was perhaps inclined to be a little grandiloquent too—though not necessarily by nineteenth century Spanish standards—when he claimed for instance that in writing his story "our head was covered with the tephilim of the Jews and our breast with the escutcheon of the Holy Office."[17] In his "Studies on the Jews of Spain," he kept harping on "the curses that rest on the brow" of "the outlawed"; and the "deicide race, ... suffering the punishment for the great crime perpetrated at Golgotha without their being able to wash away the blood that came over them and their sons"; and those "bereft of even the

remotest hope of ever ending the torments to which they have been condemned."
Yet, at the same time, he considered that "the Spanish Jews do not deserve
the hatred which the people always felt for them, nor does their literary work
merit the disdainful indifference which they have been shown until this day by
all nations," and he pleaded that the time had come to "cast off the stale
prejudices and to do justice to the many and enlightened spirits which the
Hebrew race produced in Spain."[18]

The time was indeed not far off. Even while he was writing (in the 1870s),
Amador de los Rios thought that, 25 years earlier, "nobody was remembering
the edict of 1492 . . . nor the regulations of 1802 and 1816. The laws were saying nothing nor did it occur to anybody to close the ports of the Peninsula to
anybody who might come to live peacefully among us."[19] This was true enough,
up to a point, yet as late as 1850 professing Jews were not allowed to travel
through Spain, let alone (as a general rule) live in it.[20]

The spring of 1848 sent some unsettling currents as far as Spain, and
after years which at best had "seen no advance in efficient administration,
in political stability or in civic virtue,"[21] in 1851 "a concordat with the Vatican,
[was] concluded without submission to the Cortes" by which "Catholicism was
confirmed as the exclusive religion."[22] Queen Isabella's reactionary regime was
not too rudely shaken by an upheaval that promised an approach to toleration.
In 1854 a coalition of progressive *moderados* seemed actually in command.
Soon high hopes sprang up among Jews. The Board of Deputies of British
Jews appointed a committee to explore the possibilities of a legal return. They
asked the *Consistoire* of Paris to join them in appealing to Spain, but the
French, so recently after the coup of Louis Napoleon, were apprehensive
about troubling their government on what must have appeared to them a
secondary issue, and the British chose not to attempt it alone.[23]

Rabbi Philippson's Initiative

A bold initiative, however, was taken in 1854 by a leader of German
Jewry, Dr. Ludwig Philippson, rabbi of Magdeburg and editor of the famous
Allgemeine Zeitung des Judenthums, who was pleased to have noticed "great
changes in the political and social conditions of Spain."[24] He addressed to the
new Cortes and the government a memorial (legal abstract) demanding
religious freedom in general and more especially the repeal of the decree of
Banishment. Claiming to speak in the name of "German Israel," Dr. Philippson
said:

> Far removed from the Iberian Peninsula, members of another beautiful and beloved father-
> land, of another magnificent and esteemed people, we raise our voice solely in the service
> of that great and sublime principle of whose true application, however, we Jews in all
> countries have come to be the acid test — in the service of the freedom of religious worship —

and we raise our voice also to demand from the representatives of a magnanimous nation the redress of an ancient wrong, justice for a great historical act of violence which, though it happened in a darkness far off, is still being felt today.[25]

Dr. Philippson briefly sketched the history of Spanish Jewry from the earliest times—not, he stressed, as Jewish or foreign authors saw it but according to the "unbiased" Studies (from which he extensively quoted) of Amador de los Rios who had recently borne witness that "the expulsion dealt a mortal blow to trade and commerce." The rabbi said, however, that he was not dwelling upon "the curse that inescapably follows the foot of religious persecution," nor upon "the extraordinary material disadvantages which are bound to show themselves in the wake of intolerance." Further:

> The centuries have all too plainly preached the lesson of their experience . . . though the adversary is still far from having lost his power, indeed time and again [he] manages to regain it, nevertheless he has fallen dumb; rational reasons he can offer none. Where the examples of America, France and Belgium, Holland and England, Germany and Denmark speak . . . we can say mankind has spoken, and the demand for this freedom of religious worship can no longer be refused in any country claiming to be civilized, among any people claiming to be regarded as humane.

Still, Dr. Philippson continued, Jews have a very special right to approach the highest tribunal of the Spanish nation: in the face of God and mankind, they must plead for the repeal of the Banishment edict. That plea must be granted whether the freedom of religious worship was or was not introduced, because by that repeal, Spain's ancient guilt in history would be redeemed, and also because subsequent administrations had all too often violated a general clause of the constitution under the pretext that conflicting special laws had not yet been revoked.

Was anybody fearful that Spain might be "flooded by Jews"? Not likely, he claimed. People cruelly expelled from a country are not easily tempted to return; they would not soon leave a fatherland in which they had struck roots as citizens enjoying every right. The times, the German rabbi pathetically remarked, when they had to count themselves lucky if one land on earth would receive them once another had driven them out were gone for ever. On the very day after their departure from Spain, Columbus had set sail to discover a new world, and it was in that direction that Jews were now wending their way. Dr. Philippson summed up:

> We do not come to demand the estates that were taken from our fathers, to demand restitution for the inestimable goods of which they were robbed, not even to recover the ancient temples which were once our hallowed sanctuaries and whose battlements can still be seen—we come only to blot out the disgrace of banishment, to obtain free entry for those of our faith who may wish it. It will not cost you anything except one word, but a word most dear, for it is a word of love, humanity, justice, civilization.

This memorial received the support of two French congregations which Dr. Philippson previously approached as they were nearest to Spain, those of Marseilles and Bayonne, though the *Consistoire* of Bordeaux, like that of Paris, was, more discreetly, in favor of silence.[26]

In Madrid a notable stir was created. The government paper *Novedades,* of 20 October 1854, welcomed the petition since there were no reasonable grounds for refusing it: "In terms of economics the readmission of the Jews would assure us of substantial benefits." Another paper, *Esperanza,* of 21 October, though raising no basic objections, felt uneasy. If Dr. Philippson had pointed out that Jews had settled in Spain even before it was Christian, this might tempt the Jews to claim possession of all Spain! The "foolish scare" was ridiculed in a third paper, *Clamor Público,* of 24 October. [27]

The new spirit showed itself in declarations proclaiming freedom of religious worship (*la libertad de cultos*) on these considerations: "Spain owes its decay to the religious intolerance which robbed the country of every kind of merchant, industrialist and workman and latterly brought about the most iniquitous persecution of the most illustrious men in science, literature and art. Now is the time to open the gates to so many of the Spanish race who were once outlawed and are scattered throughout the world where they help to increase the wealth of their adopted countries."[28] Others raised the fundamental issue. In a pamphlet entitled "Popular Prayers for the Spanish Nation," a writer, Luis de Asoz y Rio, declared:

> We confess before you, O Lord, the great sin of our nation committed against the descendants of the ancient people of Israel, whom our fathers treated so cruelly and at length drove out of the country of their birth without making any distinction. Pardon, O Lord, this cruelty because we repent it. And when you who are the God of Abraham lead back his sons into Spain, let us not forget that you say to them "I will bless them that bless you and curse them that curse you".[29]

However, the *moderados* did not prosper. No more than "a first timid approach to religious freedom"[30] had been attempted, and even the little proved too much. The "tolerant spirit" was drowned in a wave of clericalism that sought to "make the Catholic unity of Spain a political and intellectual reality."[31] Dr. Philippson was unofficially told that any action such as he had in mind would provide the opposition with "a banner for civil war"[32] (which was probably no mere excuse), and within a matter of months, the old regime was in bloom again. Accordingly, the Cortes referred the German Jewish plea to a parliamentary committee, and on 28 February 1855 they produced a charter, Article 2 of the Constitution, which however was never promulgated.[33] Dr. Philippson found himself left as "a crier in the wilderness."[34]

The queen and her friends, supported by the clergy, bankers and small shopkeepers, maintained staunch opposition to anything like religious liberty. In those days, Europe was "from time to time scandalised by acts of intolerance" in Spain.[35] The "tradition of the Inquisition" was, for example, seen in a new Spanish press law which threatened police action against any attempt to proselytize for any religion other than Roman Catholicism.[36] Nevertheless, some changes were noticeable. The Spanish government began to show a benign interest in the fate of Jews outside Spain. Jews in Morocco saw hopeful signs in Spanish policy. In 1860 the *Jewish Chronicle* wrote: "God be thanked, the sufferings of Jews at Tetuan are at an end. The Spaniards are in possession of it, and there is not the slightest doubt that the Jews will be most efficiently protected by the humane conquerors."[37]

Four years later Spanish consuls in Morocco were instructed to use their influence for the protection of the Jews against cruelty and injustice from the local "Moorish" authorities.[38] The Madrid directive was hailed by the *Jewish Chronicle* as "one of the most remarkable documents in modern Jewish history" since it was "the finest manifestation of sympathy with the sorely tried Jewish race exhibited by Spain for the last five centuries." Even more was seen in the document—"an implied acknowledgement of the wrongs inflicted on the Jewish people and an admission of its innocence . . . a striking proof of the extraordinary advance made by Spain on the path of liberalism," showing that Spain "has finally and completely broken with the iniquitous past by its own repudiation." Thus, "the ancient hatred of the Hebrews" was now clearly "extinct in the highest social spheres. . . ." The *Jewish Chronicle* then asked, "who among us does not know the power of example when set in the most exalted quarters and the irresistible influence exercised by it on all classes of the population?" At this time in 1864, Sir Moses Montefiore was in Madrid on his way to the persecuted Jews in Morocco, and the *Jewish Chronicle*[39] wondered: "Would the appearance in Spain of the most illustrious son of the patriarchs not afford a most desirable opportunity to the Government for effacing from the statute book of the kingdom laws reflecting the darkest of centuries . . . which, to this day, render it illegal for a Jew to establish his permanent abode on her soil? Will not Queen Isabel covet the distinction of repairing the wrong committed by another Queen Isabel?"[40]

The matter was actually broached at a meeting of the Board of Deputies of British Jews where Sir Moses, their president, was asked to raise it in Madrid; but the plea went unsupported, for reasons which the *Jewish Chronicle*[41] took pains to set forth: of course it was a matter not only of "right and justice" but equally of "sound policy and common sense." "No Spaniard will deny that soon after this ruthless expulsion of the Jews the first symptoms of national decay manifested themselves in his country. . . . A mind that is bigoted in religious matters cannot conceive any large ideas in art, science, politics or in fact in any other direction in the domain of the spirit." Unfortunately, the article continued, prejudice was still "deeply rooted in Spain";[42] only recently a liberal paper had been prosecuted for praising religious tolerance as favorable to the promotion of colonization there. The trouble was the influence of the Roman Catholic priesthood whose dislike of Jews was only surpassed by their hatred of Protestants; Jews might be regarded as harmless pests but Protestants seemed a positive peril. There was a point in the argument that once toleration was granted to one group, how could it be withheld from another?[43] So the Jews' prospects were dim. Still some inroads had been made. Professing Jews are known to have settled in Seville as early as 1860,[44] and in 1865 the Paris *Consistoire Central* obtained permission for French Jews living in Spain to have their own cemetery, though they were not to erect any religious building in connection with it.[45]

Jews had been able to return to England, and the *Jewish Chronicle*[46] drew comfort from the example. If Jews came back in 1655, it was not by demanding an immediate repeal of the expulsion decree but only "after due preparation of the public mind." Menasseh ben Israel had "chiefly craved permission for his coreligionists to form a congregation possessing all those institutions marking a Jewish community and enjoying the protection necessary for the safety of their persons, property and the exercise of their worship, and ultimately was satisfied with the hint given him that although the enactment of any special decree was inexpedient, yet no obstacle would be thrown in the way of their settlement." Through that procedure, the *Jewish Chronicle* explained, "the thin end of the wedge" had been driven in, and a similar course might be pursued in Spain: "Before all, Spain's liberal press should be induced in sober language, and discreetly, to broach the admission of Jews into the country and thus familiarise the population with the idea"; government action might soon follow and the Spanish Jews "would then watch their opportunities, as we English Jews have done, and they in process of time would work out their own emancipation, as we have accomplished our own."

The Revolution of 1868

It was all a little optimistic perhaps as befitted the early Victorians, but events seemed to justify great expectations. Within four years, in September 1868, the mild upheaval of 1854 was followed by an almost revolutionary tremor which toppled the monarchy. Isabella fled and now the prospect of religious liberty definitely improved. "Zealous agents of evangelical societies"[47] became more conspicuous, and once again Jews recalled their rights. This time, French Jews, foremost among them the *Consistoires* of Bordeaux and Bayonne, submitted a petition in which they said:

> We, the descendants of ancient Jewish families from Spain and Portugal, who fled to France as a result of the persecution the doleful memory of which has been transmitted

from generation to generation, have been deeply moved by the recent events in your country.

Our chief desire is to pay homage to the generous *élan* which has led you to proclaim the sacred principle of religious liberty. Anticipating that the nation, through its constitutional Cortes, will be able to give this principle solemn and enduring expression, we respectfully address ourselves to the Executive Power which has taken the initiative in revoking all restrictions, and we beseech you to complete your work by repealing the Edict of 1492 which doomed the Jews of Spain to exile.

Our fathers labored during many centuries for the prosperity and glory of Spain. Outlawed, they took to France, England, Holland, the Spanish civilization, language and literature, and it seems fair to say that in these countries their descendants enjoy a standing that does honor to the ancient homeland.

In granting our request, you will perform an act of reparation which will be one of your most precious titles to the esteem of the public and the praise of posterity.

Our request is not that of an interested party. We are French citizens, and we shall never wish to leave a fatherland to which we have become attached by three centuries of a protection which was never belied. In addressing ourselves to you, our sole purpose is to discharge a pious duty towards the revered memory of our ancestors. The names of the signatories are Spanish names: permit us to hope that they will be regarded as one more claim to your patriotic sympathy.[48]

Similar pleas were made by German and British Jews, and they all found a sympathetic hearing. The government paper *Novedades* encouraged them: nothing would stand in their way. It said, "there is no reason why the Jews should not worship without hindrance the God of Isaac and Jacob who is the same God as ours."[49] (The omission of the God of Abraham is not clear). German Jews were allowed to build a synagogue in Málaga,[50] and though it is not known whether a *minyan* was available, Marranos would easily have made up more than the necessary number.

In October 1868, the new Prime Minister, General Prim, stated: "I am convinced that the triumph of the revolution must bring about, without any restriction, every religious liberty," though he added it was not for him to grant it by his own authority.[51] A few days later, the Minister of Justice and Grace, Romero Ortiz, told a cheering crowd that "religious liberty is henceforth a fact in Spain," moreover:

The Provisional Government has abrogated the edict of the fifteenth century which expelled the Israelites from Spain. The Provisional Government has authorised the Protestants to raise a temple at Madrid. Henceforth, by the side of the Catholic church the Israelitish synagogue may be built, by the side of the Catholic church may be built the Protestant temple, and all Spaniards and strangers who may come here will be able to worship God according to their creed. It is sought in vain [he went on] to disquieten consciences and to charge the Government with being anti-Catholic — a Government which is sincerely and profoundly Catholic; a Government which is more truly Catholic than the hypocrites and perfidious ones who only yesterday called themselves neo-Catholics. It is in vain, gentlemen, that at the door of every church they have caused to be signed a protest against religious liberty, in order to impede the Government in its onward march. . . . Citizens, a cheer for the nation! for the Government of the People! a cheer for religious liberty!

The *Jewish Chronicle* commented: "It is to be noted that the Minister gives precedence to the Synagogue before the Protestant Temple, and as nobody can know how long these men, so identified with tolerance and progress, will remain at the helm of affairs . . . let us hasten to exercise the right so generously granted to us. Let us hasten to lay the foundation of a synagogue in Madrid."[52]

A few days later, on 1 December 1868, in reply to an inquiry from the now more articulate Kehillah of Bordeaux, the president of the (still provisional) government, Marshall F. Serrano, Duke de la Torre, declared that "inasmuch as the September revolution has proclaimed the freedom of religion, it goes without saying that the Decree [of 1492] is revoked."[53] This statement may have had something to do with an address presented to the government by the British Board of Deputies, though at the time it was thought to have been "favorably received but without visible effect."[54] However, the issue now lay wide open, and it was stated in clear terms by the Madrid correspondent of the London *Times:*

> The religious question requires a different solution from that mere toleration which, to a certain extent, has been for many years admitted in Rome itself. Religious freedom must be a right, not a favour. Without unbounded freedom of faith and worship, there can be no other freedom. Such is the principle unanimously put forward by the Spanish people as represented by all the *Juntas* which constituted themselves as the interpreters of public opinion on the very outbreak of the revolutionary movement. I do not know how far that principle may be followed up to its utmost consequences; but I think that, without its full development, the whole scheme of national emancipation is likely to turn out a chimera. Whatever Spain is, the priests have made it. If Spain is to be anything different, the work of the priests must be undone: men must be allowed full freedom to undo the priests' work. There must be not only freedom of conscience and freedom of worship but freedom of enquiry, freedom of propagandism, a footing of perfect equality.[55]

The *Times* Correspondent went on to ask the crucial question: "Is the revolution that Spain desires to be merely political or is it to be also intellectual and moral?"

> Is it merely toleration or is it religious freedom, as the people have proclaimed, that is going to be established? Is every man to have a free conscience, to pursue free enquiry, to enjoy free utterance, to denounce what seems to him error, to promulgate what he thinks truth? One of the Liberal journals has begun the publication of Renan's *Life of Jesus*. There is no doubt that the liberty of the Press will be unlimited. . . . Protestants and Jews will have their chapels and synagogues here as they have in Rome. . . . Whatever, in short, has been achieved in Italy, whatever has been for years the rule in France and Belgium, may be easily obtained in Spain; but there is a long way from all that to free propagandism.

The *Jewish Chronicle,* as usual, was optimistic.[56] It saw "every likelihood" that the edict of 1492 would be revoked: "The principle upon which it was based must crumble to dust so soon as the free air of the nineteenth century is let in upon it." Yet, the paper could not help reflecting, "its revocation will be opposed to the utmost by the reactionist party in the new republic." They would conjure up the bogey of an "inundation by the returning exiles." This of course was against all common sense, since "the love of the old home grows fainter, until . . . its historic associations fade into traditions. A new patriotism springs up, as was the case with the Puritan Fathers who . . . laid the foundations of modern America." But even if Jews were to come back, would Spain be the loser? So, whichever way the reactionary cry was taken, it was equally weak and futile.

Great also was the rejoicing of American Jewry. The New York *Jewish Messenger* hailed "the powerful overthrow of the Jesuits and of fanaticism" and cheered "our Spanish brethren, once again proud citizens of a brave and chivalrous kingdom." Since "revolutions never go backwards," it was thought, "what power exists, at this stage of the world's history, again to drive them forth from home and country?" American Jews were called upon to raise funds for the assistance of a Spanish resettlement, thus showing that they "have not forgotten their 'fatherland'."[57] Other Jews were less sanguine. The *Alliance Israélite Universelle* counseled caution, though in Britain their "fears were felt to be groundless."[58] Some Spanish reactionaries, spreading their views in scores of pastoral letters, circulars, and petitions,[59] declared religious liberty to be incompatible with the Spanish character which was said to feel an "invincible antipathy" to the Jewish race; rehashing a whole catalogue of antisemitic legislation since the earliest times, they insisted that Jews could not and should not be tolerated in Spain.

Yet, there were confirmed advocates of religious liberty among the reactionaries, even among the priests. One of them, Victor Pamagua y Castuera, declared in a letter to the government: "Not only do I not detest religious liberty; I seek it with all my heart in the interest of that religion of which I am a priest. Catholicism is at present the first victim of religious intolerance. Through it Catholicism would perish by the worst death—the death caused by inanity and contempt. Only religious liberty can restore to her that life and energy required by her in order to rule the consciences of her enemies and consummate the great work of human unity." Another writer boldly asserted: "Religious liberty is ancient in our country and intolerance modern."[60]

Emilio Castelar

Perhaps the most powerful champion of religious liberty was Emilio Castelar, a president of the First Republic. In a famous speech in Parliament on 12 April 1869, during the debates on the constitution, he indicated the two ideas which "never succeeded yet in the world — one religion for all and one nation for all. Illustrious Pontiffs tried from time to time to accomplish the first but failed. Alexander, Caesar, Charlemagne, Charles V and Napoleon tried to accomplish the second and likewise failed. The idea of variety conquered the conquerors. The variety of consciences conquered the Pontiffs, and the variety of people conquered the warriors." He then denounced the "religious intolerance that began in the middle of the fourteenth and in the fifteenth century," when a sermon in Toledo's Cathedral had caused the massacre of 3,000 Jews there. Castelar went on: "In depriving herself of the Jews, Spain deprived herself of an infinity of names who might have been the luster and the glory of the country"; he named Spinoza whose "glory might have gilded our horizon," and Disraeli, "the head of Britain's aristocracy."[61] To those who in their resistance to religious liberty went so far as to threaten "disbelief in Christian doctrine if the Jews returned to rebuild the Temple of Jerusalem,"[62] he said: did they believe that the Jews of today were the Jews who "crucified Christ"? Did they believe in the terrible dogma that the children are responsible for the sins of the fathers? "I do not believe it. I am more of a Christian than that! . . . Great is the religion of Power, but greater is religion of Love. Great is the religion of implacable Justice, but greater is the religion of pardoning Mercy. And I, in the name of that religion — I, in the name of the Gospel, come here to ask you to write in the front of your fundamental code: Liberty, Equality and Brotherhood amongst all mankind."[63]

In the ebb and flow of this debate which left no doubt that "the whole political philosophy of the revolution stood committed to the freedom of religion,"[64] the Cortes, eventually, on 6 June 1869, proclaimed the new constitution whose Article XI declared:

> The Catholic Apostolic Roman religion is the religion of the state. The nation undertakes to maintain its worship and its ministers. No one shall be molested or persecuted on Spanish soil for his political opinions nor for his particular form of worship so long as he keeps within the bounds of Christian morality, but no other ceremonies and no other public manifestations than those of the religion of the state shall be permitted.

The constitution also laid down, in Article XXI, the *libertad de cultos,* providing that "the nation undertakes to maintain the worship and ministers of the Catholic religion. The exercise in private or public of any other religion is guaranteed to all foreigners resident in Spain without any further limitation than the universal rules of morality and law." The same was to apply to any Spaniards professing a religion other than Roman Catholicism.[65]

These declarations, passed by a majority of 164 to 40 (with 76 Republicans abstaining),[66] notably, if guardedly, differed from previous constitutions (1812, 1822, 1834 and 1854) which upheld the supremacy of the Catholic Church, with no conceivable image beside it. Dr. Philippson and his friends were pleased with the result; they congratulated Spain on the "magnificent victory over her past"; the question was, would it last?, and the answer seemed by no means certain. Even now some felt that by tolerating other religions, the constitution "disinherited Catholicism".[67] Yet the revolutionaries of 1868 were no frantic iconoclasts, any more than republican *sansculottes*; they were essentially realists, and though some tended to deny dogmatic religion or would occasionally even announce in very modern terms that God had died, nevertheless they could not but appreciate that the Church in Spain was very much alive, fortified by the stringent doctrine of the first Vatican Council then in session, and their best prospect was in fighting the claims of the Church by the sanctions of the state.[68] Thus, on the whole, the constitution of 1869 was, in its relative merits, quite an achievement, and "only those who knew Spain before the revolution could appreciate the importance of the change that had taken place."[69] Of course the letter of the law was dependent on the spirit of its interpretation.

How much of the old spirit still survived, was indicated by a Madrid correspondent of the *Jewish Chronicle:* "The Jews are still represented ex cathedra as impious deicides, as enemies and haters of Christianity, as occasional slaughterers of Christian children, as blaspheming Jesus three times a day, etc. These infamous calumnies . . . are taught to this day by ignorant priests and find no contradiction. . . . Foreign literature, periodical or other-wise, has scarcely access in Spain. . . . It is said therefore, that while this ignorance prevails . . . it would be imprudent to make an ostentatious parade of public Jewish worship which might lead to an outbreak of popular fanaticism and to a consequent disaster."[70] Of course no such plan was put forward, but it was suggested that an effort be made to enlighten Spanish opinion by taking advantage of the now unfettered press "with a crowd of cheap newspapers published throughout Spain."[71] They were to carry a series of articles "containing an able exposition of the principles, ethics and practices of Judaism, adapted for popular comprehension." In that way, it was fancied, "many errors and prejudices would be in time eradicated and correct views formed, much to the advantage of the future Jewish communities in Spain." In fact, two isolated attempts had already been made. Spanish papers printed a "Letter" from Gibraltar and another from Bayonne in defense of Jewish tenets attacked.

The effect of such enlightenment was, even then, notoriously uncertain. To a very large extent it was as true then as in 1864 when the *Jewish Chronicle* said it, that "The mass of the Spaniards is not yet ripe for this reversal of ancient policy."[72] Fanaticism had certainly "given way to feelings of a quite different order," at least "in the highest social spheres," but there was a kind of searing skepticism which saw "obvious contradictions." Amador de los Rios was much impressed by "the Spanish clergy's consistent protest in the name of Catholic unity, and their determination not to rest in its defense." He asked, "What can the descendants of the Spanish Jews hope to gain from

the new law in view of the mournful and terrible lessons which their history
on Iberian soil teaches them and given the explicit and unequivocal protest of
the clergy? Time will show." As an historian, he felt "anguished and uncertain"
at the sight of a "provocative and aggressive revolutionary Parliament inspired
neither by the maturity nor the caution or moderation which the great
humanitarian ideas require in order to bear good fruit in their natural
growth," nor, he added, did those in the opposition camp reveal that "spirit
of charity which, springing from the pure and life-giving fountains of the Gospel,
bring about the greatest social transformations and work the greatest wonders
in history. Sensible men, he continued, far from any petty interest and burning
passion, free from all political or religious fanaticism, looking upon the events
of the day with a serene mind and a tranquil heart, do not see and cannot
see any clear sign suggesting that any solution has been found to the problem
posed in the Cortes by the Jews of Germany in 1854."[73]

Coming as it did from a supposed enlightened historian, it was not a
particularly encouraging assessment but it was a realistic one. Little changed—
under one government or another, Conservative or Liberal, Royal or
Republican. Between 1869 and 1875, twenty-five Jews were naturalized.[74]
By the end of the century it was recognized that Jews, in common with
other foreigners, could obtain naturalization on any of these five grounds:
(1) Marriage to a Spanish woman; (2) the establishment of an important factory
in Spain; (3) the possession of land which pays direct Spanish contributions;
(4) the practice of a trade with one's own capital, and (5) the rendering of
eminent services to the country.[75]

Occasion was frequently taken to stress that, in accordance with Article
XI, no one was to be "molested" because of his religious beliefs,[76] and as a
new constitution was being discussed, one of the issues became once more the
place of religion in Spanish history. "To conservatives, religious unity was
synonymous with Spanish greatness; it was not her shame but her glory that she
had remained isolated and immune from progressive but 'dissolvent' ideas from
Luther to Voltaire. Tolerance was the demand of revolutionaries who wanted
to destroy the Church in the name of progress and in the interests of a minute
sect—the Protestants, consistently favoured by English and American money."[77]

"Catholic Unity" versus "The Modern Age"

The Church tried to retrieve the power that she had lost. After all, the
constitution of 1869 did qualify the Concordat of 1851, and in November
1874, King Alfonso XII introduced himself in a somewhat unorthodox formula
as "a good Spaniard, a good Catholic and a liberal"[78] (even if not necessarily
a "good" one). But when the Nuncio made "vehement" representations on the
restoration of "religious unity,"[79] the government gave the "conciliatory reply"
that they "would conform to the Pope's demands within the limits set by the

internal conditions of the country."[80] In fact, "Catholic unity, if desirable . . . was conceivable only in a society where the Inquisition was acceptable and efficacious," and the government could hardly resist pressure, chiefly from Britain and Germany, in favor of Protestants' rights.[81]

However, the then reigning Pope, Pio Nono, was not a man to be treated lightly. On 4 March 1876, he addressed a letter to the head of the Spanish Church, the Cardinal Archbishop of Toledo, declaring that it was not only the idea of freedom of worship that had to be banished from Spanish soil but equally "the funereal evil of the proposed tolerance"; the Spanish bishops were exhorted to defend "the cause and the rights of the Catholic religion." The Pope's thrust was parried with the prompt revelation in the Cortes that during the negotiations on a "settlement of the religious question," His Holiness had "accepted religious freedom in Spain as he accepted it everywhere else."[82]

About the same time, on 3 April 1876, while the constitution was still being debated, the Anglo-Jewish Association submitted to the king a memorial praying that "those who hold the faith of Israelites shall not be debarred, on the score of such religious profession, from any of the rights which may be granted to the adherents of any other religious denomination.[83] A similar petition was sent by the Board of Deputies.[84] British Jews enjoyed the goodwill of representative public opinion. In a powerful leading article, the *Times* declared that not only "all educated Jews must seek the abolition" of the Expulsion decree but "educated Christians" too "because the persecution of the Spanish Jews and their banishment form one of the darkest stories even in the records of intolerance." The Jews' demand was "particularly interesting at a time when the Vatican is attempting to revive the institutions of Spanish intolerance," and indeed "so intense is the rancour of the clergy against heresy and so great is still their influence that the Ministers must go gradually towards toleration." However, the *Times* went on, the Spanish government:

> dare not shock the moral sense of Europe. . . . The practical result even of dogmatism like that of Rome is determined by the moral atmosphere of the age. . . . The moral influences of our time have made even the most recklessly Orthodox feel that the decrees of the Inquisition and the expulsion of the Jews were miserable blunders. . . . What Spain imperatively needs today is not more orthodoxy but more freedom, so that her people may be quickened at every turn of their lives by competing agencies. She might become richer, quieter and better educated if a large brigade of her idle and superstitious clergy could be exchanged for an equal number of active, pushing traders, fearless men of culture and zealous heretics, whether Protestants or Jews.[85]

After prolonged parliamentary debates, a modus vivendi was found. Catholicism continued to be recognized as the religion of the state, but equally the private practice of all other faiths continued to be tolerated. This was hardly progress, but it was probably as much as could be expected in a society in which it was possible for legislators to argue that while "not adherents of the Inquisition," they "accepted the spirit of it."[86] The Liberal Prime Minister,

Práxedes Mateo Sagasta, bluntly told the vociferous opposition that they "had to come to terms with the modern age, even if we introduce religious unity." To refuse to do so, would be like "destroying the railways, closing our ports, converting the factories into convents — in other words, shutting ourselves off from the civilized world."[87]

The same point was made by the Conservative leader, Cánovas del Castillo: "Are we to oppose ourselves to the concert of European nations, when our position in Europe, in America and Asia makes it necessary for us to secure the sympathies of the entire world? . . . We have to compromise with the whole universe."[88] One of the Liberal chiefs, Romero Ortiz, one-time minister of justice, proposed an amendment authorizing the public and private exercise of every form of worship whose religion was within the universal rules of morality and right. The idea was to give clear expression to the principles of liberty of worship professedly conceded by the government. The amendment was defeated however by 190 to 33. So was, by 226 to 39, a reactionary amendment. Shortly after, emerging from a rough passage, the relevant clause was adopted by a majority of 221 to 88. It took care to keep a balance by omitting to go farther than its predecessor. In fact, the constitution which came into force on 2 July 1876, retained Article XI; it was after all "the nearest approach to a tolerant society which Spain had known."[89]

Some Jews were disappointed by its "obscure and ambiguous language,"[90] but the *Jewish Chronicle* was satisfied, being certain that "the formal repeal of the edict of Banishment" was now "only a matter of time"; it derided the "motto of the clericals — Catholic unity" which admittedly had "a charm for the everyday Spaniard of which we here in this country amidst a Babel of sects and creeds have no notion," but what this "sham" really meant was "Catholic uniformity" which was "too often a base coin . . . deceiving the multitude by its factitious resemblance to the genuine metal. . . . The very appearance of [Catholic] unity must have deserted long ago a country which has given birth to a Castelar and the glorious liberal school of which he is so distinguished a leader." As for Jewish immigration, the paper urged, it "should for a time be slow and circumspect," and since most would probably emigrate from such backward regions as Morocco, it should be given the benefit of "salutary educational influence" by "some civilising agency."[91]

Any concern that might otherwise have been felt, was allayed by the Prime Minister Sagasta, who said Jews could "come to Spain without any obstacle whatsoever, being sure that the Government, interpreting the opinion of the country, will receive them with kindness and sympathy."[92] When, at the end of the second Carlist War in 1876,[93] the American Jewish Board of Delegates, through the United States ambassador in Madrid, congratulated the king on the restoration of peace, "praying that his reign might be signalised by a formal revocation of the edict of 1492," Sagasta described Article XI as "the most decisive revocation."[94]

The Spanish government actually offered the memorable spectacle of inviting those who were then fleeing from tsarist persecution. Almost immediately, in June 1881, it threw "open the doors of what was once their ancient land" (*recibirán a los Hebreos procedentes de Rusia, abriéndoles las puertas de la que fué su antigua patria*).[95] The phrase was perhaps a little unfortunate since, strictly speaking, few of the Russian Jews would have qualified[96] — more likely those of Rumania and Bessarabia — and certainly expectations in Madrid of 60,000 being allowed to settle wherever they liked were grossly exaggerated.[97] Some papers welcomed the offer as "a service to the nation which in importance was without parallel in this century."[98] The Spanish ambassador in Turkey had high hopes of the "immense" commercial advantages his country would reap and so he boldly suggested both a regular shipping line between Odessa and Seville, and also the promotion of Spanish teaching at new Spanish schools in Constantinople and Salonika. In the event no more than a handful landed at Barcelona in September 1881, and though ten years later, Jews in Odessa actually asked for "repatriation," they seem to have had second thoughts.[99] The "batches of Russian Jews, totally unfit for the experiment" who were "dumped into Madrid by the organizing committees in Germany,"[100] soon moved elsewhere. Barren as it was, the incident could hardly fail to stir deep emotions. By her "wise and liberal offer," the *Jewish Chronicle* wrote, "Spain has at last publicly acknowledged the error and injustice of barbarous intolerance"; after all, "for nearly 800 years Spain was to the Jews another Palestine, and even since the expulsion they have continued to look back on it with feelings but little inferior in tenderness to those with which all Jews regard the Holy Land." Ever since the revolution of 1868 efforts had been made to secure the Jews' right of settlement in Spain: "This has at last been granted and no time could have been chosen more opportune for the favour than the present when the need for a friendly asylum is felt by all Jews of Eastern Europe." Their recall to Spain would lead to a "rejuvenescence" of the country, because "a good action is its own best reward" and "other more substantial advantages" would be provided by "grateful Judaism in the world of commerce."[101]

A very different view was taken by the principal German Jewish paper, the *Allgemeine Zeitung des Judenthums,* whose editor, Dr. Ludwig Philippson, had been foremost among the champions of the Jews' right to enter Spain. He now thought indiscriminate immigration had "dangerous aspects."[102] Apart from being racked with corruption, the country had not accepted "the spirit of tolerance and the need for freedom of conscience." The reason why Jews were called to Spain was thought to be materialistic rather than idealistic: the country needed capital and Jewish enterprise, and while of course no matter for reproach, this showed that "any immigration of poor or less well-to-do Jews would put them at a grave disadvantage, if not in peril" — except perhaps in ports, with a bigger volume of trade, where people were used to the presence of strangers.

The German Jewish paper found its views confirmed by a leader of the

Alliance Israélite Universelle, Isidore Loeb, who had advised settlement "only for industrialists and businessmen with more or less substantial capital"; small traders would be unable to make a living because of the fierce competition. Accordingly, no progress was made by a Spanish Committee for the Promotion of Jewish Immigration which was founded in July 1886 by Senator Isidoro Lopez Lapuya, and even the vigor of Emilio Castelar who headed a similar committee could not change the facts of Spanish life.[103]

Beginnings of Jewish Settlement

The number of Jews in Spain hardly grew and it was exceedingly small. The census of 1877 identified 406 — 276 males and 130 females — in a population of 17 million; in Cadiz alone there were 125 males and 84 females. For "Madrid Province" the figures were given as 17 and 14. In Madrid itself a correspondent of the *Jewish Chronicle* in 1876 knew of "probably 120" mostly German Jews, also 60 French Jewish families, and five years later the same paper referred to "some hundreds." In 1884 Madrid Jewry was stated to consist of "nearly 30 families";[104] Seville also was believed to have 30 (mostly Moroccan) families, with a synagogue, a Jewish school and a cemetery.[105] There were a sprinkling in Toledo, Alicante, San Sebastian,[106] Irún, Huelva and Rio Tinto, and about the year 1900, the estimate for the whole country was 2,000.[107]

While some were small traders, especially jewelers, slipper makers, importers of dates and honey, exporters of olive oil[108] (mainly in Seville), most were affluent—merchants, representatives of mercantile houses, entrepreneurs, bankers, who lived in Madrid, Barcelona, Málaga, Cadiz. Many of these came from southern France and Germany, though very few were concerned about their Judaism; they lived and were known as French, Germans, Austrians, Swiss.[109] As early as 1834, Daniel Weisweiller, a strictly religious Jew, established himself in the banking business of Madrid and soon struck up a partnership with a fellow-Jew, Ignacio Bauer, and their firm acted as Rothschilds' agents.[110] By 1868 they had achieved sufficient standing to lend the government 400 million reals.[111] Weisweiller also was Austrian consul as well as representative of the German city states of Bremen and Lubeck.[112]

In 1843 the Jewish firm of Frois, Silva, Blanc and Co. set up a textile factory in Vergara (Basque country). In 1855 Silva Bros. did the same in nearby Villabona, and Messrs. Rodriguez and Salcedo started not only a textile factory in Tolosa but also a paper plant in Irún.[113] Alfredo Salcedo soon opened a bank in Madrid,[114] as did Jules Gomez and Co. who became the main agents for the sale of French textiles in Spain, and in 1860 a German Jew, Leopold Lehman, was actually elected president of the Bank of Madrid.[115]

Their main involvement, however, was in the quickly expanding railways. Between 1848 and 1858 some 500 miles of railways were opened, and in the following ten years another 3000. Foremost in this essential and lucrative business were again Weisweiller and Bauer. The construction of the Madrid-Irún(-Paris) railway was financed by the Pereire brothers, Emile and Isaac, and Isaac's son Eugene, while Emile's son, who was also named Emile, was administrator of the Northern Spanish railways.[116] Their headquarters were in Paris with boards of straw directors sitting in Madrid. Their interests extended "from discount banking and insurance to coal-mining, brick-manu-facturing, sugar-refining and gas works."[117] Another banking family, the Camodos, had railway interests mainly in the south (Andalusia).

Such religious life as was possible was fostered by the Salcedos and Bauers. In Madrid, in contrast to Seville, it was not considered prudent to build even a humble synagogue, but rather to wait until events had shown that Jewish worship would be absolutely protected. Therefore, prayer meetings were held in the privacy of drawing rooms especially on the High Holidays,[118] and Bauer became the quasi-acknowledged leader of the Madrid community. His wife was prominent in social life; her "handsome and richly furnished" salons were a rendezvous of the literary and artistic avant-garde.[119]

On the whole, however, it was probably true that, in the second half of the nineteenth century, "most Spaniards hardly knew what a Jew was." As a result of centuries of Church indoctrination it was hardly surprising that feelings unfriendly to them were still strong, though perhaps no more than in some other European countries at the time. Edouard Drumont's book *La France Juive* was translated into Spanish by a priest Rafael Pijoan, and another partisan of the Church militant, Peregrín Casabó y Pagés, produced a mediocre equivalent, *La España Judía*.[120] A Franciscan, Fr. Angel Tineo Heredia, sought to justify the expulsion and denied any benefit to be derived from the Jews' return.[121]

Others again offered more "modern" arguments, and since the so-called "Jewish Question" served more and more to mark the divisions between Progressives and Conservatives, reactionaries would hold the Jews responsible for the growth of freemasonry, while those who claimed to stand for "law and order" accused the Jews of "dangerous tendencies."[122] Some Jewish families who had settled in Toledo were actually driven away by the "fanaticism and intolerance" of the people. Even in Madrid, a priest, "moving in high circles," presumed to denounce "aristocratic ladies who associated with Jews," but he was promptly transferred to a less distinguished post. The incident was optimistically considered "sufficient to show the great regard entertained for the Jews."[123]

Dr. Angel Pulido Fernández

An unusual token was a striking initiative taken to revive such links as Spain once had with Jewry, and they were discovered among the descendants of the early exiles, those Sephardim who still spoke a basically native medieval Spanish, Ladino, in many lands across the sea as well as around the Mediterranean in Greece, Turkey, and North Africa. Their story found a champion, as unexpected as remarkable, in a Christian Spaniard, Dr. Angel Pulido Fernández, a physician, one-time government inspector general of Health, secretary of the Academy of Medicine, and a prolific writer on medical matters; he was also a (Liberal) senator representing the University of Salamanca.

Pulido met Ladino-speaking Sephardim for the first time in 1903, when aged 51, on a cruise along the Danube. He was amazed to hear from them, in his own ancient language, about their far-flung congregations in the Balkans, and upon his return he began to plead for government action to "protect" the Spanish spoken in the East.[124] In February 1904 he published six articles in the Madrid paper *La Ilustración Española y Americana*, and a few weeks later, on 29 April, a book entitled *Los Israelitas Españoles y el Idioma Castellano*. In this book which aroused immediate attention, Pulido said he hoped to "put myself in touch with the Jewish people and to obtain the necessary data for a better understanding of the important subject and so to present it more appropriately to my country." The book accordingly contained a questionnaire designed to elicit the maximum information on the Sephardim all over the world.

The response was sufficiently encouraging for Pulido to persist. A year later in 1905, on the basis of the information supplied, he wrote another book, the very substantial *Españoles sin Patria y la Raza Sefardí*. This magnum opus, contained a survey of (a) the Sephardic people in general, (b) Sephardic communities in each country, and (c) an assessment of "Spain's future relations with her ancient sons" (p. 12). Pulido asked: Did Spain lose by the expulsion of the Jews? Ought she to seek reconciliation with the descendants of her children? (p. 527). The answer to the first question was obvious to him. Spain had suffered both materially and intellectually; that much was "a truth enshrined in the conscience of all Spaniards, whatever their religious beliefs." He thought "a bloody amputation was inflicted on the body of the nation" and "all the vital interests which are today at the center of the political economy, the nerve system, the blood and the muscles of modern nations, were most certainly, most sadly crippled" (pp. 529-34).

At the same time, Pulido realized the obstacles in his way. There were still, he wrote (p. 1), "ferocious resentments and antagonisms," "negative spirits," "poor and hardened hearts" (p. 524), especially in the Roman Catholic Church (p. 541). At best he found himself derided as "a new Quixote." He was not however dismayed. In the first place, he enjoyed the goodwill of reputable papers such as the Republican-Democratic *El Liberal* and the Conservative *España* (p. 521), for he considered his endeavor as one in the larger battle between "the liberal and the reactionary spirit" (p. 215), challenging "the cruelty of ignorance" (p. 549). Spain had few friends; she was suffering "the greatest of her history's disasters," and here was a singular opportunity to resurrect some of her greatness (p. 550).

The reference to the "greatest of Spain's disasters" was no figure of speech, for only seven years earlier, Spain had lost the war against the United States. In a material sense she lost the last of her overseas possessions; the year 1898 "marked the end of the second cycle in Spain's history that had begun four centuries earlier." To some the loss of the remaining colonies came "as a relief from a nightmare." But in the self-esteem of the country, this was a "moral disaster," "a most grievous hurt, and the humiliation prompted a mood of self-introspective analysis among her serious thinkers, later to be known collectively as 'the generation of '98'."[125] Curiously enough, Pulido does not mention the debacle of 1898. It is enough for him to know that Spain is in a lamentably backward state, which he describes in great detail, and thus he argues a reconciliation with the Sephardim could not but act as an "ethical" and "spiritual" tonic (p. 534). "We want Spain to become for them once again a land of grandeur and of glory. . . . Let Israel be in no doubt [he writes a year after Herzl's death]; the time of her resurrection has already begun. We do not know whether her Zionist hopes will be fulfilled. We do not know whether this concentration of her life in a small state will be of benefit to humanity and to the Hebrew people. What we do know is that the Jews are today occupying important positions all over the world . . . and that Jewish blood, nerve and brain will be a vital factor which will never be overcome by all the hatreds of barbarism nor all the crimes of fanaticism."

While many Sephardim welcomed the campaign in theory, others were distinctly reserved; they were Orientals of the East, they said, and would remain so.[126] Besides, they asked, was Pulido's really the authentic voice of Spain? They would not believe that Spain had turned as tolerant as Pulido made it appear. The Ghost of 1492 was still besetting their minds. Pulido was at infinite pains to reasssure them: that decree had completely lost its validity (p. 217). The nineteenth century had "a very different national soul" than the fifteenth (p. 537). Could anybody possibly doubt this? (p. 557). Nor was it fair to say that popular feeling was at odds with the spirit of the modern laws. They, who thought of Spain as "a land of Roman Catholic fanatics," knew little about her, for there were "few nations where feelings of religious unity have more disintegrated." It was true a large section of the country still wore "a conspicuously clerical garb," but another substantial one was "passionately irreligious"; lots of people "simply resigned themselves to toleration of the extremists on both sides," and the largest number were more or less avowedly indifferent (p. 217).

Certainly, Pulido thought, there was nothing similar to populist antisemitism in Spain; he had never met a single Jew, either a visitor to Spain or a resident engaged in business, who had ever been molested or suffered any indignity because of his religion or race. There was definitely nothing like that "mass of infamies and falsehoods" which went by the name of *L'Affaire Dreyfus* (p. 562). The "disease called antisemitism" was unknown in Spain "because we don't feel any envy or distrust on account of Jewish monopolies or moneylending or predominance" (p. 218). Seeing that his purpose was to create conditions in which envy, and so forth, might well be felt (because of the presence of Jews), he did not realize how soon, upon his own showing, antisemitism might cease to be unknown.

Perhaps indeed Pulido was a little naive, as naive as the ethical optimism and the never-wavering belief in human progress which was the hallmark of the nineteenth century. Those, the doctor said, who "fear the rise of a new Tor-quemada in the person of a Cabinet Minister" merely "prove that they know noth-ing of a constitutional law in a country constitutionally governed" (p. 558): "Neither a Royal Order nor a Royal Decree issued with the authority of the executive, nor even a ruling by the legislative chamber under the Crown, are able to modify a constitutional law which would require a special session of Parliament endowed with the highest power under the Constitution. None could either detract from or add to the tolerance proclaimed in Article XI." The only thing possible was that "the country, international usage, greater culture and cosmopolitan life increasingly consolidate in the conscience of man that respect on which rests the peaceful living together of all who profess different creeds." Therefore, Pulido went on, why bring up the past: "the liberal spirit of the nation and the winds of reason from abroad have between them extinguished for ever the ancient fires and put an end to barbarism" (p. 559).

Nor was Pulido any more impressed by those who suggested possibly em-barrassing interpretations of Article XI. What if the government and courts were to discover that the clause about "the respect due to Christian morality" might be given an interpretation very different, for example, from Sagasta's and "leave the field wide open to arbitrary contention?" (p. 559). Well, the "Christian morality referred to" in the text was none other than "that universal morality of every civilized people that will not allow its good customs to be offended, its feelings of shame assailed, on excuses which strike at the law and conventions of an honorable society." If this were not enough, there were still the Ten Commandments and the Sermon on the Mount!

Pulido's dedicated effort did not go unnoticed outside Spain, though hardly beyond the Jewish fold, and there it was granted little more than the esteem bestowed on every lost cause. The German Jewish historian Meyer Kayserling, himself an authority on the Jewish story in Spain, baldly dismissed the first book as "the product of a missionary that merits no further notice."[127] Another German Jewish scholar, Dr. Martin Philippson, the son of Ludwig, urged upon the Sephardim "extreme caution" and he drew a truly forbidding picture of "the fanaticism and the Spanish people's hatred of the Jews" which would "make life impossible for Jews there." After all, he said, the few Jews who had settled in Spain were not allowed to reveal their identity since this would almost certainly mean "outlawry not only by the rabble but also by the vast majority of the educated." The mere thought of building a synagogue was out of the question, and "even if government and Cortes were to permit large-scale Jewish immigration, the all-powerful priesthood and the populace incited by them would render it illusory—a fact which even the noblest intentions and fairest promises of individual friends of the Jews would be unable to change."[128]

Another critic, a Madrid (Jewish) correspondent of the *Frankfurter Zeitung*, had some kindlier feelings. He had noted everywhere a "sympathetic interest" in Pulido's ideas, though admittedly also much indifference. Any immigration of Jews, he thought, would render "an inestimable service" by compensating for "the enormous emigration of Spaniards each year." Though aware that it was "a good Spanish tradition always to talk a lot without acting upon it," he had been pleased to hear of a proposed all-party propaganda committee to initiate (particularly commercial) contacts with the eastern Sephardim and eventually set up a "Hispano-Jewish Congress."[129] The German correspondent blamed the Spanish authorities for having neglected opportunities which since had been seized by the alert *Alliance Israélite Universelle* to spread the blessings of French civilization. He could not understand the inactivity of "Jewish colonization societies and well-known philanthropists," since, in his opinion, "the Spanish-Jewish question" had now "entered a decisive phase."

Max Nordau, himself of (distant) Sephardic descent, dismissed the idea that the Sephardim would be "sufficiently interested to return to Spain and trouble to find out what she was like." He thought Pulido should not bother to correct an "historical error": "Spain must in this matter open a new account, as they say in business." He did however pay tribute to "the generous and gallant book, yes gallant too, because it is well known that there are still people in Spain today—and not a few—whose mentality is not very different from that of those who expelled my forefathers four centuries ago."[130]

One of them, a professor of Canonical Law at the University of Valencia, Dr. Joaquin Girón y Arcas, actually wrote a pamphlet in reply to Pulido entitled, "The Jewish Question in Spain and the Sephardic Race," in which he asserted: "If all the Spanish believers were readers of the Bible, as is desired by Dr. Pulido, the Jews would be even more unpopular in Spain than in fact they are" (p. 63). He in turn was answered by an English resident near Barcelona, Ms. Isabel Lawrence, in a brochure entitled "Salvation must come from the Jews," showing that all Christians are in duty and charity bound to treat the Jews well. With this argument the author upset some diehard churchmen, and the Vicar General of the Bishopric of Salamanca, Dr. D. Ramón Barberá, gravely warned the faithful to avoid the "absolutely heretical and scandalous" thoughts, "under pain of mortal sin."[131]

However, the government had little time for this mentality. Wherever possible, they gave signs of goodwill. Some tangible evidence was mentioned by Eliezer Ben-Yehuda, the Hebrew scholar living in Jerusalem: "The Spanish Ambassador in Constantinople officially invited many Sephardic Jews of that city to a banquet on board the Spanish warship which was then in the Bosphorus, and during the banquet the Ambassador and the Commander of the ship made speeches full of warm praise of their 'faithful brothers', the descendants of those whom Spain had 'mistakenly' exiled."[132]

Ben-Yehuda deprecated Jewish suspicions that "the new friends of our people in Spain" might not be "acting quite unselfishly"; perhaps they were not, he wrote, but

> this material aspect of the movement, the existence of which I cannot doubt, does not much affect its value in my judgement. It is a recognised principle of modern politics that there is no friendship between nations so lasting as that which is based on community of interests. If the Spaniards have now got so far as to seek the friendship of the Jews because of the advantage which they expect from their return to Spain, that is a very good thing. Friendship based on so substantial a consideration will endure, at least as long as its basis — the advantage which Spain will derive from the Jews — remains: and that, we may hope, will be a long time. Hence, from this point of view alone, we have no real cause to oppose this movement.
>
> Nor ought we on moral or psychological grounds to refuse to treat this movement with respect. No doubt the recollection of the expulsion from Spain is extremely painful to the Jew and fills him with bitter indignation. It is a chapter in our history of which the memory will not soon be wiped out. But if we are to shun every land which has drunk Jewish blood, every country in which we still have to suffer persecution day by day, then we have scarcely a place left under the sun: for what country is there from whose soil the blood of Israel does not cry aloud?[133]

The Spanish philospher, Miguel de Unamuno, who was then chancellor of Salamanca University and greatly respected Pulido, was more than doubtful: "The return of the Jews to Spain [he declared] is neither a religious nor a political problem, but solely an economic problem. I cannot imagine what the Jews could do in my impoverished country. If there is in any Spanish circles a resentment against the Jews — although I do not believe there is — it is entirely attributable to a fear of the Jews as competitors in the economic field."[134]

However, Pulido seemed unconcerned by either praise or criticism. He pursued his course with another book, *El Sefardismo en España*, in 1910, and at the end of the war, in 1920, he published one more, *La Reconciliación Hispano-Hebrea y el Pueblo Hispano-Hebrea: Primera Base Mundial en España*, of which a French translation appeared in Paris in 1923.

It is now fairly clear that the skeptics were right. Pulido's campaign had no appreciable practical effect, either among the Jews or the general public in Spain. It is even doubtful whether his "enthusiasm produced a state of mind in Spain which sympathized with [his] ideal,"[135] and he certainly cannot be credited with having "obtained in 1909 permission to open synagogues in

Spain."[136] A Hispano-Hebrew Union, launched by Dr. Pulido in March 1909[137] under the patronage of King Alfonso XIII, designed to spread Spanish culture among Jews, was short-lived and of little consequence; no greater success was achieved by such sporadic efforts as that of the Madrid Artisans' Union in urging Jews to return.[138]

Independent of Pulido's campaign, however, by the time his third book had appeared in 1910, the struggle for freedom from religious prejudice had advanced sufficiently for Article XI to be characteristically amended. A Royal Order, dated 11 June 1910, now specifically stated that religious meetings were henceforth not to be regarded as public demonstrations, and that the use of religious emblems, notices and other external signs for buildings destined for worship different from the Spanish state religion, were now to be authorized.[139]

This advance, slight though it may appear in retrospect, was "greatly appreciated by the numerous foreign missions existing in semi-concealment in Spain."[140] As recently as 1905, the Bishop of Barcelona had objected to Protestant chapels being built since "they had not complied with the law which prohibits the use of all external emblems of a religious character . . . other than those of the State religion."[141] His "violent intolerance" found no sympathy in the Spanish press; public opinion was distinctly "in favour of religious liberty being granted to all classes of Spaniards who obey the law." In fact, it was foreseen that the bishop would "hasten the advent of liberty."[142]

Nowhere of course was there greater satisfaction than among Jews. Even Dr. Martin Philippson, who five years previously had been so eloquent in decrying Spanish antisemitism, now hailed this token of "full freedom of religious worship."[143] He wrote, "the Jews too may erect publicly synagogues which can be recognized as such. They may acknowledge their religion and disseminate and advocate it without fear. And this toleration is shown not only by the government but also by the people,"[144] indeed, it had been demonstrated that "light will triumph over darkness, however obstinate darkness be in defending itself." Some were encouraged to feel that "the official clergy who do not bear much good will towards Protestants and Freemasons, recognise in the Jews a peaceful element and therefore allow them to go their own way."[145]

The spirit of friendship for Spain among Jews was shown at the time of Alfonso XIII's state visit to England in June 1905. The king then received a deputation of the London Spanish and Portuguese Congregation, led by Haham Moses Gaster, who presented a humble address of welcome. Describing themselves as "descendants of former subjects of your Majesty's glorious ancestors," they:

> recalled with profound gratitude the great epoch of Jewish history which was created by our forefathers in Spain and the ties of religion and literature which consequently bind the whole Jewish people to that fair land. . . . We deeply appreciate the generous attitude of your Majesty's Government towards religious liberty and are grateful for the liberal treatment now extended to our coreligionists in your Majesty's dominions. We sincerely hope

that members of our faith may once again form one of the elements of the great Spanish nation.[146]

The expulsion was not mentioned, and the king was complimented by the *Jewish Chronicle* for having "wisely refrained" from replying.[147] Some Jews strongly disapproved of the approach. A Budapest Jewish weekly was perhaps a little melodramatic in its comment but not entirely unrepresentative of orthodox opinion: "Oh how low have they sunk, the descendants of Spain's exalted nobility. . . . They now live comfortably off and undisturbed in a peaceful country . . . and yet they have remained slaves. . . . Have these civilized slaves no ear for the groans of all the victims of the Inquisition? How dare they express the hope that ever again Jews will settle in the land which bears the curse of our saints?"[148]

Zionists too felt that the London Sephardim had been unduly ingratiating. Dr. Weizmann chided Gaster on "that Spanish affair of his," though he gave him credit for having "rehabilitated himself somewhat" after the haham had "utilised his contacts in Spain and put pressure on the Moroccan conference to improve the situation of the Jews in Morocco, apparently with great success."[149] The Spanish government again showed concern for the 20-25,000 Jews in its Moroccan Protectorate; to those of Laraiche, for example, it presented and bore the costs of an extensive site for a synagogue and school. It also took action against local antisemites.[150]

On a larger plane, Spain intervened in Palestine during World War I when the Jews there, the majority Sephardim originating from Turkey, were subjected to harsh treatment by the Turks. In April 1917, as the British advancing from Egypt threatened to invade, all of the 45,000 Jews were to be evacuated. Those in Jaffa and Tel Aviv had already been sent to Galilee and Samaria; they were to have been deported along with those from Jerusalem to Syria and farther away into Asia Minor where they may well have shared the fate of the Armenians. As soon as this news became known, the Spanish government, responding to appeals by neutral countries including Argentina, made an "urgent" demarche in Berlin and Vienna as well as in Constantinople, "demanding an end to the persecutions, deportations and lootings practiced against the Jews in Palestine."[151] As a result, the deportations were stopped.

Within Spain, an important milestone was reached in 1910 when the first Jew was elected to the Cortes, Gustave Bauer, son of Ignacio. The *Jewish Chronicle* saw "time's revenge" in this "triumph of the *Ewige Jude*," his "reconciliation even in the land of the terrible Inquisition—[since] . . . the world does move."[152] Whether Jews should now be encouraged to go back "in a way for which some Spaniards have yearned," was a different matter. Around that time, an originally Russian Jew, Samuel Schwarz, director of an important mining concern, was elected a member of the Madrid Academy of Sciences.[153]

Shortly after, in 1913, another characteristic event occurred in a very different sphere. The (Liberal) Prime Minister Count de Romanones had just reaffirmed "the sentiments of affection and tenderness for a large number of our brothers in whose veins flows the same blood as ours and who [were] expelled in an age of fanaticism,"[154] and now his government decided to establish a professorship of Rabbinic Language and Literature at the University of Madrid; two years later, by Royal Decree of 21 June 1915, a Chair of Hebrew Literature and Jewish Learning was created: its first occupant was the Berlin Orientalist, Dr. Abraham Shalom Yahuda.

Dr. Yahuda owed the appointment to the dedicated efforts of a number of enlightened Spaniards such as: the leader of the Radical party in Parliament, Gumersindo de Azcarate; the Archbishop of Valencia, Salvador y Barrera; and more especially the Jesuit, Fr. Fidel Fita, president of the Academy of History, who had written extensively on Spanish and Spanish-Jewish history, literature and archaeology; he now thought it "an honour for us to secure Professor Yahuda." The Jerusalem-born professor happened to be of British nationality, and because he refused to give it up a special law had to be passed sanctioning the appointment. He was solemnly installed on 15 December 1915 at a ceremony where the Dean of the Faculty, Professor Tormo, declared that while he was a fervent Roman Catholic himself, his religion did not in the least prevent him from respecting the old faith of his new colleague.

Max Nordau, who happened to be present, praised the "quiet but efficient and, taken all in all, sufficiently ostentatious disavowal of a long and black historical past"; the Banishment edict had been "tacitly ignored and stamped as obsolete." The Spanish press prominently featured the event, complimenting the government on its initiative which had shown their "resolution to break with old prejudices and to follow the road of progress."[155] Some Jews were inclined to link the occasion with Pulido's exertions. "It is clear [wrote Ben-Yehuda] that the Spanish Government now wishes to pave the way for the return of the 'Spanish Jews'." He thought that Pulido and his friends had understood the Jew. "They know that the Torah is the source of his life and they, therefore, hope that a chair of Jewish learning will be an attraction for many Jews who will be able to take part in the development of culture and commerce in Spain." At the same time, the Hebrew scholar (Ben-Yehuda) felt:

> we Palestinians will have cause for regret, for we hoped he [Yahuda] would soon return to his native land and teach Jewish scholarship from a chair in the Hebrew University which is to be established in Jerusalem. But as this project has not been carried out, and there is as yet no home of Jewish Scholarship on the mountains of Zion, we rejoice that our fellow-countryman has been summoned to a position of such distinction and importance. That a Jewish scholar, and a native of Jerusalem, should be a Professor of Jewish learning in

the Spanish capital, is a fact of importance in our history. It is a pleasing and inspiring prospect.[156]

Dr. Abraham Yahuda himself took a realistic as well as a sentimental view.[157] He did not think Spain had acted merely from "platonic love for Hebrew"—any more than he regarded Pulido's ideas to go "beyond a sentimental and idealistic conception" (except perhaps among the then 20,000 Jews in Spanish Morocco, who, incidentally, inscribed Pulido's name in the Golden Book of the Jewish National Fund).[158] The government was reactionary, Yahuda thought—"as in all other countries"—and his appointment seemed "part of a design to attract Jewish settlers." The Liberals and intellectuals had been "anxious to mark their emancipation from the bad traditions of the past"; they not only wanted to gain the sympathies of the Jews and to be enlightened on an important branch of Spanish history and culture but they also wanted a revival of economic life.[159]

Part of the strictly intellectual endeavor was the furtherance of Hebrew academic interest. As far back as the 1890s, to mark the 400th anniversary of the discovery of America, Dr. Kayserling had been commissioned by the Spanish government to write his book, *Christopher Columbus and the Participation of the Jews in the Spanish and Portuguese Discoveries.*[160] Now the *Junta para Ampliación de Estudios,* the Athenaeum, the University of Madrid and other institutions organized academic courses on the life of Sephardim in various countries—"some with good success, others failures." By 1920, a *Casa Universal de los Sefardíes* was founded in Madrid, with "claims that were on the grandest scale and results, as always, scanty."[161]

Yahuda appreciated all efforts to "get full legal liberty of worship" and "to stop any interference from fanatical elements," whom he feared to be not negligible in number. For this reason, he felt, Jewish immigration would be undesirable, notwithstanding the fact that the country was "rich, undeveloped and [had] a good opening for large capital and enterprise." Jews, he thought, should wait "until the Liberals get the upper hand."[162]

His skepticism was, in some part, caused by personal experience since he was made to suffer those jealousies to which scholars seem able to add a special sting of venom. When, toward the end of the war, he began to travel abroad in the furtherance of his specialized studies which the war had made all but impossible, he was accused of neglecting his duties and prolonged controversy engulfed the faculty, press and Parliament. Matters came to such a pitch that Yahuda submitted his resignation in 1920. He was, however, ably defended by his dean, Professor Tormo, who also raised the matter in the senate. By his lectures abroad, especially in Oxford and London, Tormo said that Yahuda had increased the prestige of the new Spain which was so different from the old:

What can be finer than to enlarge our spiritual horizon in times which have witnessed the narrowing of the material limits of the territories subject to our sovereignty? We must think of that greater Spain which embraces the Sefardim of the three Continents, of Eastern Europe, Asia Minor and North Africa and calls to intellectual reconciliation and fraternal affection the Spanish-speaking inhabitants those countries beyond the Atlantic which once were Spanish.[163]

The minister of public instruction and fine arts hastened to add his testimony that Yahuda had indeed "conferred a boon on Spain, showing that we are calumniated abroad when foreigners speak of our intolerance." So the resignation was withdrawn, but not for long. In 1922, Yahuda left Madrid for good.

The professor was not the only prominent Jew then resident in Spain. In September 1914 Max Nordau arrived, virtually expelled from France as an (Austrian) enemy alien. Of "Hispano-Judaic" ancestry, he confessed that he was "dying of impatience to get to Madrid" where of course his fame had long preceded him. He "loved the country" with which he "had even deeper affinities than he himself ever realized." He knew Pulido; Romanones, the Liberal leader; José Maria Lopez Mezquita, the painter; Hoyos and Espina, the authors; the literary elite of the *Ateneo* invited him to lecture in French on "The Principles of Nationality," and the Spanish Academy of Medicine accepted him as one of its foreign members. In the five years that he spent in Spain, Nordau was as prolific as ever, contributing to the international press, and here he wrote the book *Morals and the Evolution of Man*, which appeared in Spanish in 1917 three years before the original.[164]

Nor was Nordau's Zionism forgotten. He met Dr. Weizmann, and Felix Frankfurter; Vladimir Jabotinsky came to hear his counsel. Then there were the many Jewish refugees, who

> . . . crowded about Nordau and Yahuda. Every hour those two had to intervene, help, encourage, plead with the Ministry for the persecuted or the needy. Moroccan Jews came to the capital to implore protection against some Spanish consul who, Fascist before the word came up, had bullied and insulted them in every way. They received satisfaction in that the consul got a better job and left Tangiers. . . . Later Sefardim arrived from Salonika.[165]

Some, though threatened with deportation as "Bolsheviks," were saved through the good offices of Yahuda, Pulido, Nordau and the British Ambassador Sir Arthur Hardinge;[166] others were turned away despite pleas by the same friends in Spain, as well as those by Nathan Strauss of New York, and the Chief Rabbi of Buenos Aires (Halphon).[167] Many Sephardim were helped by Pulido to obtain Spanish citizenship during the war.[168]

The First Synagogue

Meanwhile the general atmosphere was judged sufficiently favorable to enable the official opening of the first synagogue in Madrid. It was not much of a place, even though in the center of the city, near the Puerta del Sol—"a dark apartment going out on a court yard,"[169] on Calle del Principe, 5 (second floor), with accommodation for about 100. Its members hailed from 18 different countries, including Argentina, Mexico and Persia, and most were wartime refugees.[170]

> Nordau, the unbeliever who had written *The Conventional Lies of our Civilization,* clad in a *tallit* and with covered head, solemnly accepted the honor of carrying the Scrolls of the Law to the Tabernacle. He did it as a matter of solidarity, of strengthening the bond that held together this poor community of exiles. But out of the abyss of the past, out of the centuries of continuous harboring that one ideal, the ideal that puts the Torah above everything else, rose the soul of his people, and the daring thinker, the intrepid visionary became humble in the presence of the people's Torah. A deep emotion forced to his trembling lips the prayers he had almost forgotten.[171]

The consecration of *Midrash Abarbanel* took place on 3 February 1917.[172] It was marked, almost symbolically, by a Bar Mitzvah, the first openly conducted in Spain after 425 years.[173]

It seemed as if Spain had come of age, and though the war had done nothing to still — even in this neutral country — the emotions of enmity (only recently an Anti-Masonic and Antisemitic League had been founded),[174] a bright light was lit that, even in a dank backyard, could not be overlooked. The Hebrew shadows took on substance, and Spaniards began to hear voices far off. One of the most curious among them was the poet Rafael Cansinos-Assens. He was once present at a celebration of Hanukkah:

> Rare and dim memories re-arose in his mind. It seemed to him as though long forgotten recollections came back to life, differing entirely from the purely religious emotion. The lights of Hanukkah had mysteriously awakened in him the soul of his forebears, whom he discovered to have been converted Jews. And the Spaniard did in fact write a novel *The Lights of Hanukkah.*[175]

Cansinos-Assens also wrote a book with the history-suggesting title, *España y los Judíos Españoles,* which was in fact a *Confessio Marranica,* a collection of sentimental and philosophical reflections as indicated by its subtitle *El Retorno del Exodo.* He fervently echoed many of the views of Pulido whose friend he was, saying, "this romantic love we feel could help promote the grandeur of Spain." He also knew and translated works by Nordau; with enthusiasm he sat at the feet of Yahuda whose presence alone in Spain, he felt, had "gone far to purge our black record." He delighted to believe in "the steadily more secure progress of tolerance in our country." Eventually, he fancied, "Mother Spain will once again be the mother of Arabs and Jews."[176]

It was a fine vision, and so far as the Jews were concerned, part at least came true when the League of Nations decided, in 1920, on the Mandate for Palestine. This, to some extent, depended on the vote of Spain, and her voice was cast among those in favor. Dr. Weizmann has recorded the memorable fact:

. . . Suddenly we discovered a great deal of unexpected and — at the moment — inexplicable sympathy in Spain. Members of the learned societies, the higher clergy, prominent members of the Spanish nobility, received the local [Jewish] delegation in the most friendly fashion. Meanwhile, in London, we called on the Spanish representative of the [League] Council, and it chanced that he was to be the President of the session at which our fate was to be decided. We said to him: "Here is Spain's opportunity to repay in part that long-outstanding debt which it owes to the Jews. The evil which your forefathers were guilty of against us you can wipe out in part." Whether it was our plea, whether it was the pressure from Madrid, the Spanish representative promised us his help . . . and kept his word.[177]

Meanwhile Dr. Pulido was pursuing his campaign with unabated vigor, keeping it on the high level to which he had first raised it. The Spanish nation's "moral rehabilitation in the world [he declared], its peace with its own conscience, its return to a place of honor in the family of nations cannot be achieved without a full measure of reconciliation with the Sephardic brothers who are as much part of the great Spanish race as we who are today living within the physical boundaries of the Spanish State."[178] But he became now more painfully aware of the widespread indifference he met, to say nothing of the downright hostility of "fanatics who professed to see a plot of Jewish origin" designed to bring about an "invasion of Jewish phalanxes from the four corners of the earth." Thus, he made a point of stressing that:

the Sephardic movement has never envisaged an influx on a large scale even of Spanish Jews. . . . I never proposed that the repatriation of the Sephardim should necessarily be in the physical sense. Not only are a great many of them so situated at present as to have no need to leave their countries . . . but it must be borne in mind that Spain is in no way prepared economically or socially to digest a considerable addition to its population. My idea is rather that this repatriation and rapprochement should be one of the mind, of the heart and the spirit between my country and the Sephardim, between the Spaniards with a fatherland and those without it, so that the former may lend the prestige of their State to the dispersed brethren and the latter inject into the life of their repenting country a new stream of vigor, a new current of fresh moral values, that will take Spain out of its isolation from the universal progress and help to restore it by their innate and inherited cultural powers to the position that once was held by Spain.[179]

The thought was perhaps a little too idealistic. But there was always more to it than idealism. In June 1924 it was haphazardly suggested that a new International University in Madrid would cater mainly to Jewish students and that Jewish immigration would be welcome with a view to reviving commerce.[180] Suddenly too this material aspect attracted more tangible attention, in a way that was sure to please Dr. Pulido. In a peculiar set of circumstances soon after the end of the war, a chance arose to tackle his project from a practical point of view, and the Spanish government seized it. The Treaty of Lausanne, 24 July 1923, abolished the system of capitulations which permitted certain residents in Turkey to enjoy extraterritorial rights and protection by a foreign power (usually Britain or France). What was conceded to Turkey was in due course extended to various countries of the Balkans and the Middle East which gradually emerged from the wreckage of the Ottoman Empire. Many of the people concerned, merchants and traders, were Sephardic Jews. Now Spain felt, perhaps under the impulse of the newly established dictatorship of General Primo de Rivera, that here was an opportunity to expand Spanish influence — through those who still cherished links, however frail, with Spain. If they had lost one protection, they could be assured of another.

Approach to the Sephardim

This end was to be achieved by the Royal Decree of 20 December 1924 which provided for all "individuals of Spanish origin" who were "already enjoying protection by the diplomatic agents of Spain as if they were Spaniards" to acquire full civil and political rights if they so wished and particularly if they possessed no such rights wherever they happened to live. An official *exposición* explained:[181]

> There are abroad, mainly in the countries of the Near and Middle East and in some parts of the American Continent, people [or their descendants] who have long enjoyed Spanish protection and generally persons belonging to families of Spanish origin who, at one time or other, were entered in Spanish registers; and these Spanish elements, animated by a deeply rooted affection for Spain, have not been able to obtain our nationality, either because of ignorance of the law or for other reasons extraneous to their desire to be Spanish. Many of them have the wrong impression that they already possess Spanish citizenship and that all they need to enjoy it to the full is some external requirement . . . others expect a mass naturalization of the community of determined friends of Spain to whom they belong. . . .[182]

While both the constitution and the civil code contained provisions governing the procedure of naturalization, it was stated, in practice the difficulties in the way of potential applicants were insuperable and as time passed their situation was becoming progressively anomalous:

> For this reason, the Military Directorate . . . has had to consider remedies, not so much in order to attend to repeated requests of those who appear before the foreign Governments as quasi-naturalized and could not indefinitely remain in this uncertainty, but in deference to an urge of patriotism which appreciates that these elements generally have an expert knowledge of our language and that naturalization must make them useful instruments in the service of our cultural relations in distant lands where they form colonies which can be of undoubted advantage to Spain. As it is not possible to grant petitions for blanket naturalization by whole communities, a procedure impracticable under Spanish law, there can be no other way than individual application and separate consideration of each case on its merits.[183]

In an effort to mitigate the old fears of "mass immigration," the *exposición* added: "There is no reason to assume that, in order to make the grant of citizenship definitive and legal, the beneficiaries will immediately travel to Spain so as to renounce any other nationality and swear the oath of loyalty to the constitution of the monarchy"; the special circumstances of the individuals concerned might well make it impossible for them to come to Spain.[184]

Full rights were to be obtained on application before 31 December 1930 to any Spanish diplomatic mission in the land of the applicant's residence. Both the routine of red tape and the specific requirement of residence in Spain were to be omitted. A circular of 29 December 1924 directed all Spanish envoys to give maximum publicity to this decree. Jews were not mentioned by name; it would have been gratuitous: they were the only intended beneficiaries. The decree was of particular importance to those Sephardim in Greece who had lost their Turkish citizenship and were not desirous of becoming Greek citizens.[185]

José María Estrugo, a well-known Sephardic writer, recommended the "epoch-making event" of this "act of contrition and reconciliation," saying:

> The crimes and atrocities of the Dark Ages belong to history and should be forgotten. Spain was not alone to err. Many other nations have sinned likewise. But it is a great consolation nowadays to note that in the midst of hatred and persecution of the Jew in many a civilised country, the land of the old *Quemaderos* and *auto-da-fés* throws her doors wide open and wishes to make a place in the sun for the sons of the expelled. No doubt Spain will benefit very much by attracting to her useful and honest people, and also the good will of the Jews the world over. Needless to say those Sephardic Jews who enjoy full citizenship rights in other lands, particularly in the United States, of which they are proud of being loyal citizens, will not change their nationality. It was not intended that they should do so, and Spain will not insult them by thinking that they would. But there are multitudes of Sephardim in Europe who for one reason or another, owing to political vicissitudes and changes in the map of the world, find themselves without any legal status and are practically "men without a country". Many of them did not want to remain or become subjects of nations which are acting towards them as stepmothers, and some of them have already been divested of the privileges of citizenship by their former fatherlands and are being driven from frontier to frontier. For them the new law comes as a salvation.[186]

Precisely how many Jews acquired Spanish nationality under the decree is not known. Many applied, but then "the Ministry of the Interior announced that it had no concrete instructions concerning the documents to be presented by the applicants and consequently refused to grant the naturalizations. The position was not clarified until 1927 and when the time limit elapsed in 1930, many thousands of Sephardim lost the opportunity of becoming Spaniards as well as their protection by Spanish consular agents."[187]

Even so, the Spanish government claimed "a large number." Certainly the reservoir was considerable.[188] The largest European concentration probably was in Salonika—as many as eighty thousand—and the Spanish Consul there at the time did his best to "preserve our traditional influence" among the "active,

industrious and much respected" Sephardim who "constitute an excellent basis
for the expansion of Spain in the Near East." He pleaded for "an intellectual
and commercial expedition from Spain to visit Salonika and found there a
Spanish press, also schools and a library"; there was a great deal to do, though
he was also a little skeptical because of the "limited means."[189]

Perhaps material resources alone were not to blame. It seems fair to
assume that a great many Sephardim were not eager to draw on Spain's un-
doubted goodwill. For one thing, a demonstration of attachment to a foreign
country, albeit strictly cultural or spiritual, was open to misunderstanding.
Turkey, for example, where so many Sephardim lived was then in a severely
nationalistic mood as a result of Kemal Ataturk's reforms. The "cultural unity"
of the country figures prominently in his program and since 1925 Turkish
was the official language of instruction. The Ladino-speaking Sephardim
seemed slow in conforming to the new spirit. Therefore, presumably with some
governmental prompting, a "Turkish Unity" movement arose among them
with the slogan, "Let's abandon our corrupted idiom for the beautiful tongue
of the Gazi."[190]

Ladino was demoted to "a jargon unworthy of being spoken in Turkey."
The Istanbul paper *Vakit* was really cross: "To preserve the language of a
country which expelled them four centuries ago and to employ it in the midst
of a population which has given them all hospitality, suggests that Spain
did right in ejecting the Jews." This view, it was claimed, was "not prompted
by animosity towards the Jews who are a useful element in the country—
at least in normal times," but "all our nationals of the Jewish faith ought to
speak, read and write Turkish, so that they should be able to serve civilization
and become an important factor in the life of our country, as the Jews are in
other countries."[191]

Actually Turkish Jews speaking Ladino were liable to imprisonment.
The paper of Bulgaria's minority, *Kirkler Ili*, denounced the "exaggerated
chauvinism" of such prosecutions; in Bulgaria, it said:

> The Turkish language is heard in all places and no one thinks of forbidding the people
> to speak their national language. If the Turks in Bulgaria were compelled to use the
> Bulgarian language and sent to prison for talking in their mother tongue, hundreds of
> thousands of Turks living in Bulgaria would find themselves in a very difficult position
> and they would not stop protesting before the civilized world against this wrong to their
> natural rights. If the Turks want their co-nationals living coutside Turkey to be well
> treated by others, they should treat properly the national minorities who live in their
> country.[192]

Whether they did or did not take notice of this plea, they failed to abolish
Ladino. It continued to be spoken and was also printed in two periodicals.[193]

Some further difficulty may have been created, however, by doubts raised
over the validity of Spain's action in international law. In 1925 the editor of

the Shanghai monthly *Israel's Messenger,* N. E. B. Ezra, renounced his British citizenship and placed himself under the protection of the Spanish Embassy. In a case before the Mixed Court, the British judge refused to recognize his claim to Spanish citizenship and declared that he had remained a British subject because of his birth in India. The Chinese government to whom the case was referred decided that the Spanish consul had no right to grant protection to persons who did not originate in Spain. Judge Martin thereupon held that if Ezra were not a British subject according to his statement of renunciation, he must be subject to Chinese law. Spanish Consul General Julio Palencia officially demurred, charging the British assessor of the Mixed Court with misleading the public; but the decision was upheld.[194]

It may well be that some such incidents caused Sephardim to think twice before invoking the Spanish law. In 1931 a plan to grant Spanish citizenship to all Moroccan Jews en bloc had to be abandoned in fact because of strong opposition in the *Maghreb.*[195] Similarly, the recurrent demands for a clear revocation of the expulsion edict made no progress beyond the soothing assurance that "if the edict had not been declared null and void, subsequent laws have done so,"[196] such as the constitution of 1868.[197] The government firmly stressed its friendly sentiments. General Primo de Rivera went out of his way to declare that Spain was fully tolerant in religious matters and that the Spanish people held the most benevolent views with regard to Jews.[198]

Under the circumstances, immigration to Spain was not entirely ruled out, if only because the general Jewish situation in those days seemed to suggest it. The United Jewish Emigration Committee in Berlin, probably motivated by a desire to find an outlet for some of the *Ostjuden,* inquired in Barcelona about possible prospects. They received a severely negative reply. Spain, they were told, had "shown itself entirely unfavourable ground for Jewish immigration." The Barcelona community, it was explained, "the only one of any significance" in Spain, had been founded by a few Zionist-minded Jews. Of its ninety-five members, about eighty per cent were Sephardim brought there by the war who lived in very humble circumstances. The twenty or thirty East Europeans or other Jews in the city also had to fight very hard for their livelihood.[199]

The information was probably intended to be politic rather than accurate. Barcelona was by no means the only community of any significance, and there must have been more Jews than the ninety-five presumably registered members. The Barcelonians would not have been the first to discourage immigration of fellow-Jews. Spanish Jewry at that time was estimated at two thousand;[200] and in the absence of statistics, it may be assumed that the Jewish population was equally divided between Barcelona and Madrid.

Those in the capital were possibly better off, if the person of their leader may be taken as representative. Dr. Ignacio Bauer-Landauer, president of the Jewish community, a grandson of Weisweiller's partner back in the 1860s and son of the first Jewish Member of Parliament, maintained the family's banking

tradition but also its social status as professor of Jurisprudence, member of the
Academy of History, philanthropist, patron of one of Madrid's largest hospitals,
consul general of Finland and friend of King Alfonso. As an enthusiastic supporter of Dr. Pulido's campaign, he frequently visited Spanish communities to
propagate the idea of a new Spanish-Jewish friendship.[201] Bauer also tried his
hand at publishing. He started a *Biblioteca Hispano-Sefardí* which produced
a few titles such as Manuel L. Ortega's biography of Pulido and another on
the Jews of Morocco. Attempts to expand this field in a *Companía iberoamericana
de publicaciones* made little progress.[202]

It is probably true that the majority of Jews in Madrid did not care to be
associated with the Jewish community and communal life accordingly was
slow. The little that existed was due to the exertions of Professor Yahuda who
no doubt was the moving spirit of an early Zionist Association named after
Yehuda Halevi. Anniversaries of the Balfour Declaration were regularly
celebrated and action was taken to demonstrate solidarity with Jews elsewhere
or to organize public protest against injustices such as the pogroms in Poland.[203]
Some boldness was required, for the general atmosphere, despite the realistic
concern with the Sephardim, was not free from antisemitic currents. The "Protocols of Zion" found many believers and talk of a "Jewish-Masonic conspiracy"
was easy.[204] Even the ritual murder lie was spread — anonymously — in a book
entitled "Spain in Africa and the Jewish Peril".[205] It particularly railed against
the protection granted to Jews in Spanish Morocco and viciously attacked such
friends of the Jews as Castelar, Sagasta and Pulido whose influence was said
to be responsible for the "imminent arrival" of eighty thousand Jews from
Salonika!

Much of the antisemitism was of course inherent in the traditions of a
reactionary Church which in turn drew encouragement from the anti-Dreyfusards
in France. But much of it also was something of a foretaste of the New Left
which had little sympathy for the Church, and here some French and much
German influence was often conspicuous. A characteristic figure in this category
was Pio Baroja, the novelist. His books presented a picture of the Jews which
his nephew, Caro Baroja, described as "not very pleasant and quite possibly,
an even more unpleasant name could be applied to it." He drew on Dostoyevski
and Houston Stewart Chamberlain as well as on Voltaire, though admittedly
not all of his Jews are caricatures. As late as 1935 he could not read the German
writing on the wall, and only the inevitably mounting horror of Nazi antisemitism gradually revolted him.

More reputable writers took up the cause of the Jews — Carmen de Burgos,
Gabriel Alomar, Rafael Altamira, Francos Rodriguez — though not all in the
unequivocally ardent terms of Rafael Cansinos-Assens. One in particular,
Ernesto Giménez Caballero, showed intense interest in the Spanish-Jewish rela-
tionship, but even though on balance he probably would have considered himself their friend, he did not mind describing them as "a great revolutionary

ferment for Spain," and he thought "all the violence which the Christians inflicted on them" was "justified."[206]

The Second Republic

The ambivalence of the intellectual climate, tempered with indifference, was hardly changed when the Monarchy yielded to the Republic in April 1931.[207] The Jews felt sorry for Alfonso now an exile. He may have become generally unpopular toward the end of his reign,[208] but as a strictly constitutional monarch he had always taken pains to make no distinctions between his subjects of different origins and creeds, and on many occasions he seemed distinctly sympathetic toward the Sephardic cause—not of course so much for the sake of the Jews as in the interests of Spain. He always had his country's peace and well-being at heart. In 1931 the *Jewish Chronicle* thought that "had he merely played for his own hand he might have provoked a civil war, and the fact that he took the best means for preventing one will always go to his credit as a mark of his personal bravery and his patriotism."[209] He in particular earned Jewish gratitude during the war when he involved himself in the effort to save the harassed Jews in Palestine. Prompted by pleas from Professor Yahuda and Max Nordau, he intervened personally with the Central Powers. The Kaiser promised relief and even suggested that the Spanish government send a neutral commission to Palestine which should remain till the end of the war so as to reassure the Jews not only there but also throughout the world.[210]

Similar to the deposed king, the rulers of the Spanish Republic affirmed general goodwill toward the Jews. The president of the Provisional government, Alcalá Zamora, expressed his pleasure over the friendly sentiments of Sephardic Jewry toward Spain;[211] the "Semitic influence" was praised by him as "one of the traditional features of Spanish culture." The Minister of the Interior, Miguel Maura, a descendant of Marranos, strongly condemned religious intolerance, and the Minister of Finance, Indalecio Prieto, explicitly guaranteed respect for the Jewish religion. Those who expected a pronouncement on the decree of 1492 were disappointed. General assurances were given that the wrongs committed against Jews at the time of the expulsion would be rectified[212]—whatever that meant. The decree was just "no longer valid," said Foreign Minister Alejandro Lerroux, and in his capacity as leader of the Republican Radical party he declared that "Spain must deal with this question radically and proclaim to the entire world that the Edict of 1492 has been annulled. It would mean giving formal recognition to the great principle of equal rights for all citizens."[213] Yet, nothing was done.

Nor was immigration promoted. Back in 1925, the Spanish author, Vicente Blasco Ibañez, optimistically thought that "as soon as the republican form of government is instituted it will be easy to bring the Jews back; at present the Monarchy is the strongest supporter of the Catholic Church and will not permit the return of the Jews."[214] But the hopes were dupes. The foreign minister stated that there were no legal restrictions on immigration; it depended solely on the extent to which the immigrants would be able to find openings for themselves in the economic structure of the country.[215] This was a sufficiently potent qualification and it was hardly necessary for the Spanish consul in Cairo to emphasize that the Republican government "has no intention of encouraging mass immigration or the creation of a new national home for the Jews, as the conditions in the country would make this impossible."[216] The point was reinforced in a report by the central committee of the *Alliance Israélite Universelle* which found that immigration was not only politically unsound, but also that Spain was "not in an economic position to absorb any substantial number of newcomers."[217]

At the same time a gesture was made, in the spirit of the Nationality Decree of 1924, by arranging for the naturalization procedure to be still further simplified. A decree of 29 April 1931 provided that the time of residence on Spanish territory was reduced from ten to two years for those who were naturalized "in the Spanish American republics, in Portugal and Brazil" and "natives of the Spanish Protectorate of Morocco."[218] Further progress was ruled out by the dour resistance of the diehards in the Catholic Church who would not hear of any, even imagined, return of the Jews.[219] They were naturally displeased by the new constitution of 9 December 1931 which, in Article 26, separated Church and state[220] and solemnly declared that " . . . nationality, sex, political ideas and religious creeds are not a ground for legal privilege which the state does not recognize."[221]

Jews, on the other hand, were rather pleased, perhaps they particularly so because of the "dogmatic anti-Clericalism" which was at the heart of Republican convictions.[221] "The Spanish people," wrote the *Jewish Chronicle,* "has apparently come to see that the predominance of Priesthood or of Militarism . . . is no longer tolerable."[223] Jews as Jews of course did not figure in the new constitution, but now what Jewish life there was began to be organized. The registered members of the Madrid congregation numbered only forty-five, a motley crowd consisting for the most part of arrivals from central and eastern Europe (Germany, Austria, Hungary, Poland and Rumania). Most Jews, and perhaps the wealthiest, did not wish to be associated with the synagogue and many did not even wish to be known as Jews. Accordingly, the congregation had to struggle for survival. It could afford neither a rabbi nor a hazan. Previously

almost the whole of the communal budget was covered by Ignacio Bauer, but when he experienced a reverse of fortune it became necessary for all members to bear their proper share of the burden. Even so, the income just suffices to cover the rent and the modest wage of the beadle. The Municipality has provided the community with land for a cemetery, but whenever there is a burial, a payment of 400 pesetas (about £11) has to be made to the Municipality, and the committee does not always find it easy to raise this sum.

After the original Zionist society of 1919 had expired, another was launched in November 1934, with Ignacio Bauer as president and Dr. Georg Sachs as honorary secretary.[224]

Conditions were a little brighter in Barcelona which always "proved a much more attractive place of refuge to Jews than any other city in Spain, thanks partly to its convenient geographical situation and partly to the extensive economic opportunities that it provides." Here the synagogue in the Calle de Provenza, opened before the First World War, had about two hundred and fifty registered members, hailing not only from central and eastern Europe but also from Holland, France, Switzerland, Greece and Turkey, Morocco and Egypt. There too, however, apparently from fear that their economic interests might suffer and also from sheer indifference, many Jews held strictly aloof from the synagogue and refused to identify themselves with any form of Jewish activity. The wealthier members of the community preferred to congregate under the severely neutral name "Union Club".[225] Even so, a Federation of Jewish Communities in Spain was formed which held its first public meeting in Madrid to consider their new status.[226] A committee was convened under the presidency of Dr. Bauer and consisting of Rabbi Menahem Coriat, from Ceuta, Morocco (who was also a banker); Manuel Ortega, the writer, and Antonio Goicoechea and Hilario Ayuso.

On 1 May 1931 the synagogue in Calle del Principe was consecrated;[227] it was still in the same two small rooms above a restaurant and next to a tailor's shop.[228] It had already been legally opened on 24 December 1930, in the presence of representatives of the city's police who read out the protocol and provisional statutes of the congregation. It was said to cater to the religious needs of some thirty families.[229] The general atmosphere seemed to be a little tense because the Church was stated to be opposed to the grant of a cemetery: it was only a few weeks after the change of regime that the Jews in Madrid received a plot of land from the government. The Jews also benefited from a new decree authorizing every citizen to obtain religious education for his children in accordance with his creed. It was now possible for Jews to demand Jewish religious teachers in the general schools. They now also began to show an interest in Jewish history and literature. A project was launched, though apparently not maintained, for research in Spanish libraries and national archives; an appeal was made to the Jews of the world for funds to enable scholars from all countries to come and study the Jewish records in Spain. For the same purpose a cultural and commercial mission was to visit the Sephardic communities in the Mediterranean and Middle Eastern countries.[230]

The Republican government too showed itself aware of the links with the Sephardim established under the Nationality Decrees of 1924 and 1931. When the Minister of Justice, Fernando de los Rios,[231] visited the Spanish zone of Morocco in 1931, he made a point of addressing the Jews of Tetuan to whom he expressed the joy he felt that the ignominy and grave injustice of 1492 had been redressed; he asked them to forget the unhappy past and think only of the present and of "enlightened Spain whose intellectual development owed so much to Jewish and Arabic culture."[232]

The minister of education readily complied with Moroccan Jewish requests for Hebrew teachers from Palestine.[233] The Jewish schools in Tangiers were given a government subsidy and when, in December 1932, the grant was criticized in the Cortes by a Catholic priest on the ground that no such favor had been shown to other denominational schools, the minister of justice replied that this was a matter not of denominational interest but of "intense Spanish cultural concern" because "the Sephardic Jews in Tangiers as in Bucharest, in Sofia as in Constantinople, in New York and indeed wherever they may be, are doing what many Spaniards fail to do—preserving their ancient Spanish language." Therefore, the minister said, "we consider it our duty to protect the Spanish Israelites, the Sephardim of Tangiers." He had often been accused of being a champion of the Jews, and he wished to plead guilty: he was a champion of the Jews as of any other persecuted people.[234] Spanish citizenship was granted to stateless Sephardic families,[235] and Spanish protection was reaffirmed for those living in Egypt and Greece, though Egypt soon afterwards, in 1937, abolished the capitulations.[236]

At home, Parliament was asked to entrust the ancient synagogue in Córdoba to the Sephardic communities, especially those of Spanish Morocco which would be responsible for its maintenance, since economic assistance to any religious denomination was barred under the constitution. In moving the bill, which never emerged from the committee stage, Antonio Jaen, an Andalusian member, said:

> An ancient historical process, involving hardships which we now all realize, once outlawed this race. Each time a new constitution was given in Spain, as in 1854-1869, the descendants of those Spaniards raised their voice clamoring for their Fatherland. Now the voice of the past has been heard in a different way, but with renewed strength, as the Sephardi Jews of Spanish race, so closely linked to our history throughout the ages, to our life and civilization, no longer have to ask: we have given our answer already. . . . They have a right to something that will show modern Spain's reconciliation to the supreme principles of man and that will, once for all, put an end to a policy that inflicted wounds on them and on Spain.

Jaen paid a particular tribute to Maimonides, the man of Córdoba—"the most exalted figure of Spanish Judaism and perhaps of the whole of medieval Judaism."[237]

This was a prelude to a great Spanish-Jewish occasion, the 800th birthday of Maimonides in 1935. The notable anniversary was celebrated in Córdoba, in the presence of a large public, both Jewish and gentile, and Jewish delegates of learned societies from many parts of the world, including the United States and Palestine, came as guests of the government, enjoying every facility of

Jewish observance. Well attended lectures were given by Spanish scholars on some such subjects as "The Philosophy of Maimonides," "Maimonides the Doctor and Maimonides the Man," "Córdoba in the Time of Maimonides," and a memorial tablet solemnly unveiled said: "The Government, on behalf of the nation, expresses its homage to the immortal genius of Judaism. Córdoba, his native city, adores his memory."[238]

It was the year of the Nuremberg Laws, so there was special point in the remark of the Mayor, Señor Garrido, that the event was "a lesson to the countries still practicing the old animosity toward Jews." Spain, he said, was proud to number among its citizens many Sephardic Jews. On behalf of the Academy of Science, Literature and the Arts, Señor Jaen declared the day "Spain's day of penitence of Jewry." He recalled the expulsion—"the black spot which we wish to wipe out"—and contrasted it with the new constitution which proclaimed equality for all religions and all races. The Maimonides celebration, he said, had not only a spiritual but also a deep political significance.[239] The *Jewish Chronicle's* special correspondent felt that Spaniards regarded the study of the life and work of Maimonides as a subject of first-rate importance in their cultural history; for them Maimonides was one of their great characters and thinkers. The occasion was thought to have been deliberately chosen by the Spanish government to demonstrate its sympathy with the Jews and its detestation of the barbarous treatment meted out to Jews in certain other countries.[240]

Witnesses and victims of that barbarism were already present in Spain. Some two to three thousand refugees were received by two special committees in Barcelona and Madrid,[241] though a good many soon left again. While the government showed them goodwill, oddly enough it did not cooperate in the League of Nations High Commission for Refugees which was set up in October 1933.[242] The foreign minister declined to appoint a Spanish member because he said, "Spain is not interested in the Jewish Question."[243]

On the other hand, Spain supported the Bernheim Petition.[244] She then declared herself "in favor of the strict fulfilment of Conventions and complete adherence to the rules of the League of Nations." According to her representative Luis de Zulueta, Spain was interested in "the affirmation of the principles and methods which the League represented. From that point of view, the delegate of Spain thought it of the highest importance that the system for the protection of minorities should be applied integrally, and he was convinced that it was of advantage to all that these stipulations should be scrupulously observed." Zulueta took the opportunity to stress Spain's concern with the Sephardim: "Spain, with that wisdom which one learned in the hard school of experience today viewed with deep sympathy and to some extent with motherly interest those thousands of families who, in centuries past, had been obliged to leave Spanish territory and who, in several countries of the Levant, still spoke the Spanish tongue and carried on the traditions and preserved the memory of the country of their forefathers."[245]

In the great debate in the League of Nations in autumn 1933, the Spanish delegate, Salvador de Madariaga, spoke up for the persecuted Jews and the wider issues involved:

> We must respect the right of each country, not exactly its sovereignty—for since the birth of the League this conception is perhaps destined, slowly or rapidly, to fade away—but the right to develop its own personality and to follow its own evolution in accordance with its own genius. There is, however, a reciprocal duty—namely, to adjust the inward evolution to the outward evolution of humanity. At a time when we are endeavoring, in the international field, to ensure the peace of the world, by respect for the liberty of each people and by free discussion, it is, to say the least, disturbing, and naturally gives the impression that anarchy among men's minds is increasing, to observe the rise of movements in which the authoritarian element predominates too strongly over the liberal element; such systems can only be regarded as in decreasing harmony with the Geneva system which believes and has always believed in free discussion and in liberty. . . .[246]
>
> Today [Madariaga continued] when the Jewish question is to the fore, the Spanish Republic turns its eyes towards that great race to which it is indebted for illustrious men of letters, lawyers, mystics, doctors and statesmen. Spain believes that the attempt to be made in the twentieth century should cover the entire world and—to use the words of a famous French writer—nothing but the world, that it should embrace all men, all races, all religions, all nations.

As late as December 1936 the Spanish Foreign Minister, Fernando de los Rios, declared that, in accordance with the Geneva Provisional Arrangement of July 1936, the refugees would be granted full rights of asylum, including permission to work.[247] But he was talking in a vacuum. Already in 1933 when the Nazi persecution began, he knew that while the heart of New Spain went out to the refugees in sympathy, "we cannot encourage their coming now," for the Old Spain was "still fighting doggedly every inch it retreats," and, he added, were the government to admit Jews in any appreciable number, "the Old Spain which calls me the *Judayzante Ministro* and the *Rabbin* would lift up its voice in its powerful Press and a crusade would begin against the Jews."[248] Clearly the New Spain was no match for the Old,[249] and though the letter seemed to give life, the spirit was all but killing. The idea that Jews were "monsters with horns and a tail" was not by any means dead yet,[250] and it was the (perhaps not always warranted) fear of it that even now deterred many Jews from openly avowing their Judaism. In spite of the Royal Order of 1910 which expressly permitted all places of religious worship to display signs of their identity,[251] no synagogue was ever so identified.

Any fears might have drawn strength from sections of the "conservative" press, such as the *ABC* and *La Nación,* where the progressive spirit of the constitution was attacked as the ghost of a Jewish "world conspiracy" and "sinister influences of a Masonic International" were seen at work[252] by a "respectable" middle class increasingly resenting what they regarded as "an alliance between Jacobin doctrinaires and a dechristianised proletariat."[253] The reactionaries of the Spanish Right-wing, who understood Hitlerism as little as Right-wing reactionaries anywhere, never troubled to conceal their sneaking condonation of Nazi antisemitism in which perhaps some heard an echo of the far-off Inquisition, and the "Protocols of Zion," embroidered by Henry Ford's fantasies about "The International Jew," really required no nursing from Berlin.[254] The forgery was elaborately exposed as was the Nazi crime then unfolding,[255] though the well-meaning minister of education did not exactly help matters when he explained that Spain needed friendship with the Jews "because of their world-wide influence, especially in finance."[256]

During the first general elections under the Republic, in November 1933, when the anti-Socialists won, Jews, Freemasons, Marxists and Catalans were pilloried as jointly responsible for all revolutionary disorder,[257] and in the elections of February 1936 these "paranoid charges"[258] became so virulently antisemitic that the shocked Jewish leaders protested to the prime minister as well as to the civil governor of Madrid.[259] The then just arising *Falange Española* made no bones about their sympathies for Hitler,[260] and their propaganda was of course stepped up with the outbreak of the Civil War on 18 July 1936. Hitler's book *Mein Kampf* had already appeared in Spanish in 1935;[261] the anonymous translator commended the Nazis' "constructive and pacifist" ideology. Now, in a second edition (Avila, 1937), the translator spread his admiration evenly over "Hitler, Mussolini and Franco, the political guides of the new Europe."[262]

The Rise of Franco

Franco was cut from a very different cloth. He was neither as wicked as Hitler nor as foolish as Mussolini. He was no antisemite, certainly not from conviction like Hitler and fortunate in that opportunism never reduced him to the straits of Mussolini. He was of course in an invidious position once he had agreed to accept the corrupting assistance of Nazi Germany, and the respectable Dr. Jekyll had only himself to blame if he were mistaken for the abominable Mr. Hyde.

In April 1937 he boldly declared: "In the religious sphere we stand for that great and comprehensive spirit that allowed, when the unity of our nation was being wrought, Mosques and Synagogues to stand open in accordance with the spirit of the Christian State." It was probably correct for his press officer to deny any anti-Jewish character of the Spanish National Movement, if only on the specious argument that "an anti-Jewish policy in Spain presumes the existence of a Jewish problem which does not exist in this country." Franco's speeches of 1 October 1936 and 19 January 1937 were cited as evidence

that "there is but one exclusion in the programme of the New Spain—
Bolshevism."[263]

Occasionally the Nationalist press would carry a message that sounded, if
only by implication, almost pro-Jewish. In January 1938 the authoritative
Noticiero de España[264] published an article by Pio Baroja who "calmly and
methodically refuted Hitler's antisemitic race theories" (though without once
mentioning either Hitler or the Nazis)[265] and shortly afterwards, on 26 February,
the paper lavished lyrical praise on Hitler's latest speech.

> The message of these articles was contradictory only to those who had done their labelling
> without considering the evidence. Franco was accepting German help and knew he was
> going to need more of it before he was through with the Civil War. It was therefore
> good politics to create a Nazi-looking party. . . . But this did not mean that he would
> accept dictation from the Nazis and still less that his regime would absorb patently
> nonsensical theories about Jews and Aryans.[266]

Still, the show he put up was bad enough. As early as August 1936, the
head of the "National Government," General Cabanellas, denounced "Free-
masons, Jews and similar parasites";[267] the paper of the Falange, *Arriba España,*
vowing to fight "International Jewry" as well as "Marxism, Separatism,
Freemasonry,"[268] freely used *Stürmer* cartoons[269] and the slogan "Spain
Awake!"[270] Even much later, Radio Burgos thanked the *Stürmer*—this
"Champion of Truth"—for its "sympathy with the Holy Cause of National
Spain."[271]

Hitler's book was translated again and went into eight editions.[272]
Henry Ford's book was also translated. Nazi antisemitism was praised by one of
Franco's foremost military aides, General Emilio Mola,[273] and General Lopez
Pinto, military governor of Burgos, proclaimed a war against "the enemies of
Christ"—the Jews and those "camouflaged Jews," the Freemasons who "must
all be destroyed without any pity."[274] One of the leading nationalist papers,
Correo Español (Burgos), promised to reintroduce the Inquisition now refined
by an alliance with Portugal and the Moslem countries "to combat the Jewish
spirit and to keep their territories *Judenrein.*"[275] Franco himself in 1939 felt a
"deep understanding for the measures taken by certain countries against the
Jewish race,"[276] and he did not mind sending his photo, with a personal
dedication, to—Julius Streicher.[277]

One man in particular was given free rein to taint the Nationalists with
the reek of antisemitism; he was the notorious "radio general" Gonzalo
Queipo de Llano. His regular broadcasts from Seville[278] were riddled with
abuse of "Jews, Masons and Marxists."[279] He declared, "Our fight is not a
Spanish civil war but a war for Western civilization against World Jewry."[280]
This war, he said—the war started by Franco!—was one "Jewry was waging on
the whole world," and the Jews hoped to win it because they had won a
similar war in Russia.[281] In his ravings he produced the most amazing tantrums

of calculated insanity. All Jews, he cried, were subject to a secret council known as the *Kahal*; they gave ten per cent of their earnings to this *Kahal* in order to facilitate the coming of the Messiah. Since there were sixteen million Jews in the world, they had paid, over the past eighteen years, 1,440 million pesetas to the *Kahal*. Even assuming that only fifty per cent had paid up, the *Kahal*'s total income was over 26,666 million pesetas. Altogether, he calculated, the *Kahal* had received 4,181,399,952,000 pesetas, and all this money was spent on supporting communism and the promotion of revolutions. On these grounds, he felt entitled to fine the Jews of Seville what must have seemed to him the modest sum of 138,000 pesetas, threatening serious reprisals if the money were not paid.[282]

The propaganda had dire effects among the thirteen thousand Jews in Spanish Morocco. Vicious antisemitism in the press bore signs of German inspiration; speeches by Goebbels and Streicher, as well as miscellaneous anti-semitic pamphlets, were widely disseminated in both Spanish and Arabic.[283] Franco at first sought to calm feelings by asking Tetuan Jewry to disregard the broadcasts from Seville. They were however to pay a price, literally—a "voluntary" contribution of half a million pesetas to the Nationalist cause.[284] In fact the Jews both at Tetuan and at Ceuta[285] were frequently mulcted of large sums,[286] and the oppression continued.

Jews were wantonly accused of profiteering from the war, and a rigid economic boycott was enforced. Jews were obliged to lower rents on their property by thirty-five per cent; but the effect boomeranged: Spanish and Arab property began to stand empty while everything owned by Jews, being so much cheaper, was rented. Special hardship was caused to the strictly observant Jews by a ban on the import of matzos,[287] and fears of arbitrary imprisonment as a means of extorting "ransom" weighed heavily on all. Tetuan Jews pathetically hoped their brethren in the International Zone of Tangiers might prevail on the Italian consul in Tetuan with a view to obtaining some relief from the Franco administration and the Arabs.[288] In Spain itself, a department store in Saragossa founded by Jewish refugees was closed and the firm's property confiscated.[289] A measure of relief was forthcoming early in 1938 when Queipo de Llano's broadcasts were stopped because of the bad impression they had created in the United States and Britain.[290]

At the same time Jews were also suffering under the Republican government, not indeed as Jews but as members of a well-to-do middle class which found no favor in the eyes of a Left-wing regime that made property "the object of expropriation for social utility."[291] The government and the Workers' Committees would seize businesses, establish a monopoly of foreign trade and nationalize large firms. These measures were bound to affect Jews, especially many of the recent immigrants including refugees, and soon after the outbreak of the rebellion, about one thousand left Barcelona for their native countries of Turkey, Rumania, Bulgaria, Austria, even Germany.[292]

In Barcelona, too, the Jews thought it wise to close their little synagogue, though only for a short time, and when in October 1937 the Minister of Justice, Manuel Irujo, announced the reopening of all churches in Republican Spain, he said that Jewish services had been held without interruption for about a year. In 1938 the community actually established a rabbinical court under Rabbi Menahem Coriat, formerly of Ceuta, though by then the congregation had been reduced to one thousand (and to five hundred a year later). In Madrid however the synagogue stayed closed because most of the relatively few practicing Jews had left that city.[293]

In view of the rather unpromising developments there was perhaps some irony in the assurances given a little earlier by another Minister of Justice, Garcia Oliver, on "possibilities of immigration"; there was room for, perhaps, twenty million, he told the Warsaw Bundist paper *Naie Folkszeitung*, though there would have to be "economic reforms designed to make the most of Spain's natural riches."[294] Above all, he said, they must readmit the Sephardim and so rectify the wrong done to them by the old reactionary Spanish regime. By contrast, the Spanish Chargé d'Affaires in Holland, José Maria Semprú y Gurrea, was more matter of fact: Jewish immigration, he felt, would depend on the international situation and the final outcome of the civil war.[295]

The victory of Franco was of course bound to arouse the gravest fears. When the Barcelona synagogue was closed down by the new authorities, the act seemed symbolic of the end of Spanish Jewry since it certainly was a clear breach of a promise given by Franco two years earlier.[296] If this were done "in accordance with the spirit of the Christian state," what sort of a Christian state was this? Admittedly it was not, despite the Nazi association, a racial state, but its Christianity was highly old-fashioned. Jewish marriages and burials were prohibited, so was the right of circumcision; Jewish babies could not be registered without baptism and Jewish children were compelled to attend Catholic religious instruction in public schools or go without any education.[279]

Presently, in December 1939, the old "Protocols" appeared in another edition, and a new version of the old hoax invented a "Council of Spanish Rabbis" which would almost certainly have secured Jewish world domination had it not been frustrated, in the proverbial eleventh hour, by General Franco. History textbooks began to shower praise on Ferdinand and Isabella for their "radical solution to the Jewish question,"[298] and though occasionally friendly gestures were made,[299] a good many Jews now left Spain for Portugal, fearing ever closer links with Nazi Germany.[300]

These fears, however justified they must have appeared under the circumstances, were in fact largely unfounded. Franco took great care not to commit himself to Hitler. The temptation was strong and at their memorable meeting at Hendaye on 23 October 1940, Hitler employed all the arts of his charisma and the glitter of his *Blitzkrieg* to win the prize of a Spanish alliance. But "he completely failed to establish that ascendancy over the Caudillo which he never failed to exercise over the Duce."[301] For once the Führer had to admit defeat. In his characteristic fashion he abused Franco as a man who "obviously does not have the stature to cope with Spain's political problems," being no more than "a Moroccan carpet dealer."[302] Ribbentrop, the Nazi foreign minister, cursed "that ungrateful coward Franco who owes us everything and now refuses to join us."[303] The plain fact was that "at a time when Hitler had tricked, bullied and mesmerised half the leaders of Europe, Franco stood out as the one man who ever took Hitler for a ride."[304]

Rescuing the Persecuted

Yet, having dared so much, Franco decided to make a balancing show of compliance by way of such expedients as a token force to fight in Russia and the abracadabra of antisemitism. These gestures helped to keep up a screen behind which as much good work was done as was perhaps possible under the circumstances. The work concerned the rescue of the Jews fleeing from Nazi persecution. If attempted as an effort to demonstrate independence from Germany, it was difficult during the years of Hitler's ascendancy, up to 1942. Even then no legal distinction was made between Jewish and non-Jewish refugees. On the whole, the policy was (1) to accept refugees provisionally and then permit them to stay on; (2) to intern those who had arrived illegally, special consideration being given to those who were not of military age; and (3) to stipulate that the refugees must not become a burden on the government's material resources and damage Spain's delicate position between the Allies and the Axis.[305]

In the summer of 1940, after the downfall of France, nearly one thousand refugees, mostly Jews hailing from various parts of western Europe, entered Spain.[306] They arrived without Spanish transit visas and frequently without other valid documents. They rarely were refused on that account: transit visas were usually issued,[307] and Spanish and Portuguese ports were permitted to serve as the then sole escape route from Nazi Europe. This good deed would make sure of its own reward, legitimate or otherwise.

> The Spanish authorities, while outwardly hostile, were not insensitive to the profits which could be made from the passage of refugees. Few who possessed funds were interned, despite their illegal entry, and all but a few were quickly embarked from Spanish ports, or sent to Portugal for embarkation from Lisbon. . . . Spanish border officials were able to make considerable sums by charging for illegal entry permits and the like . . . [also] from the beginning of the war, Spanish ship owners had progressively increased their passenger rates. By the fall of France they were charging extortionate prices for overseas passages.[308]

In this way, twenty-five hundred refugees a month were able to leave for the Americas.[309] Other refugees, among them twelve thousand Jews,[310] were interned in the Miranda de Ebro camp where conditions were extremely harsh. At that time, no Jewish relief organization was allowed to operate in Spain but some assistance was rendered by the American Red Cross which spent a total of 2.5 million dollars in Spain during the first half of 1940. This charitable work had to contend with the hostility of the Falange press which denounced the "Masonic, Jewish and Liberal" action as being "in the service of England."[311]

Not until the summer of 1941 was an official delegate of the American Jewish Joint Distribution Committee (JDC), Dr. Samuel Sequerra, recognized as a virtual consul for the stateless, operating in Barcelona; and in January 1943 a "Representation in Spain of the American Relief Organizations," headed by David Blickenstaff, began to function in Madrid.[312] As the war grew in extent and intensity, especially after the United States had taken up arms, the situation of the refugees stranded in Spain became more precarious. A contemporary report says:

> It is almost impossible to obtain the release of those who are interned in concentration camps under horrible conditions. And there is little hope that an appreciable number of those at liberty will be able to leave, since the extension of the war to the Western Hemisphere has virtually cut off all transportation facilities. In fact, the Spanish Government had deprived them of some means of transportation even before the entrance of the United States into the world conflict. Thus, as early as last October [1942], the Government administrator of the Spanish shipping line *Compania Transatlántica,* operating the *Magellanes* and the *Marques de Comillas,* without further explanation notified steamship agencies that the line would no longer accept Jewish passengers. Jewish relief agencies in Lisbon made every effort to obtain a revocation of the order which placed additional obstacles in the way of refugees travelling to Cuba; the postponement of their departure would have resulted in the expiration of a number of visas so difficult to procure. Virtually all of those left in the country had to be maintained by the American Joint Distribution Committee, which estimated the number at three hundred in its report issued in July 1942.[313]

Their number increased substantially when the deportations from France began. The border at the Pyrenees was closed in July 1942, but even so, by May 1943, some eight thousand Jews were believed to have entered Spain, all of whom were imprisoned. About three thousand were reported to be in Barcelona, the rest, in six or seven smaller towns.

> The Spanish Government refused to issue exit visas to Jewish refugees between the military ages of eighteen and forty. But by posting guarantees for their maintenance, the JDC succeeded in securing freedom for many internees, chiefly women and children, who had been held in city jails of Madrid and Barcelona, and in the camps of Miranda del Ebro and Figueras. In May [1943] the gates opened up for all Polish nationals of non-military age and later for one hundred and ninety stateless persons. At the same time, it was announced that one thousand more refugees were listed for release. These men and women were permitted to live in "assigned residence" centers where they remained under supervision but retained a degree of personal liberty. In June, three hundred and

twelve fugitives from France were released at the instigation of the American consul and sent to Portugal from where they will go overseas.[314]

By the end of 1943, the number of Jewish refugees in Spain was put at no more than 2,300.[315] 1,200 were stateless, mostly of Austrian, German, Polish and Russian origin; 500 were Polish citizens, 450 French and 150 Belgians, Czechs, Dutch, Yugoslavs and other Allied nationalities. Of these, 1,000 were in Barcelona, 300 in the Barcelona region and 700 in Madrid; 300 were interned in the Miranda camp, though after 1943 Jewish refugees making their way into Spain were no longer interned unless they were of military age.[316]

All things considered . . . the condition of the Jewish refugees in Spain was fairly good. Enough money to live on was furnished by the Jewish relief organizations, mainly the JDC, or by agencies of the various Allied nations. . . . Except for those in Miranda, many refugees found Spain, especially Barcelona, a not entirely unpleasant place in which to stay before they could return to their homes, above all in France. Proximity to France, providing a vantage point from which to follow the battle in Europe and to return right after the war, was one of the chief reasons why nine tenths of a projected convoy of nearly four hundred decided to remain in Spain and not to go to camps in North Africa. Another reason was the natural preference for freedom of movement in a city like Barcelona to sequestration in a Moroccan camp.[317]

Spain also saved some Jews by applying the decree of 20 December 1924 which permitted Sephardim to acquire Spanish nationality without actually living in Spain. Of such Spaniards in 1940 there were about 4,000, the majority in France (about 3,000), some 600 in Greece, 120 in Bulgaria, 107 in Rumania and about 100 in Yugoslavia and Hungary. When the question first arose, in Rumania in 1940, the Spanish government firmly stated that Spanish law recognized no discrimination among its citizens on grounds of race or religion.[318] This stand was reaffirmed in November 1940 when the Spanish government warned Vichy that the Jews of Spanish nationality had to be treated as Spaniards. On 7 March 1942 the Spanish diplomatic mission in Paris received definite instructions to defend Sephardic interests, and in July 1942 the Consul General there, Dr. Bernardo Rolland, informed the commissioner general for Jewish Questions: "Spanish law makes no distinction as to religious creed, consequently it recognizes the Spanish Sephardim, though of the Jewish religion, as Spaniards. I shall be obliged if the French authorities and the Occupation authorities will take note of this fact and accordingly refrain from applying to them the laws concerning Jews." As a result, Sephardic Jews did not have to wear the Yellow Badge and their property was exempt from "Aryanization."[319]

Through the same intervention, the Spanish ambassador saved Jews from despoliation and deportation, and similar action was taken by the Spanish ambassadors in Sofia, Athens and Budapest. "Spain's representatives realized that if they abandoned some of their citizens for reasons alien to the ideals of justice and morality, they would abandon immediately the dignity and prestige of the whole nation."[320]

Under the pessure of events, when the Germans insisted on neutral countries withdrawing their nationals from German-occupied territory, Spain changed her policy from protection to "repatriation"[321] albeit at a very slow pace. This was to operate particularly in respect to the Spanish Sephardim in Salonika whose number was estimated at 600. When on 1 April 1943 a branch of the Falange party was opened in Athens, the Germans tried to get the Spanish government to withdraw those Jews to Spain. The Spaniards did not want to accept so large a number then (which is probably why the offer was made in the first place); apparently they would take no more than about 50 (so they said). In Berlin a member of the Spanish Embassy told the Germans that his government would much rather transfer these 600 to German jurisdiction—if only "one could be sure that they would not be liquidated." As an interim arrangement, the Germans then proposed the transport of the Jews to some camp in Germany (Belsen.)[322]

Actually 365 Spanish Sephardim from Salonika[323] (as well as 135 who had fled to Athens) had already been sent to Belsen. On 14 December 1943 the Spanish Embassy in Berlin was instructed to negotiate the liberation of all Sephardim in Belsen with a view to having them transferred to Barcelona; the Spanish Sephardim in France had previously been allowed into Spain. On 22 December 1943 the secretary of the Spanish Embassy in Berlin requested that all Spanish Jews be "treated as Spanish citizens and be permitted to emigrate freely, for they were after all neutrals and no enemies of Germany."[324] In a note to the Spanish government dated 18 January 1944, the German Embassy in Madrid complained of this request, stating that it was impossible to segregate the Sephardim from the rest. However, on 7 February 1944 the 365 Salonika Sephardim were able to pass through Spain to Palestine via Casablanca.[325] On 9 February, 259 more arrived at the Spanish frontier, including 162 Sephardim, followed, on 13 February, by another 983 from Belsen.[326]

As Germany's power declined, Spain began to extend her protection to non-Spanish Jews. In war-torn Budapest, the Spanish Embassy issued 300 "temporary" passports to descendants of Spaniards and about 2,000 "letters of protection" certifying that their bearers had relatives in Spain and for this reason were entitled to Spanish protection. Permission was also given for 500 Jewish children to be taken to Tangiers.[327]

Generally speaking, Spain now served mainly as a channel of escape for Jews from Nazi Europe. The World Jewish Congress War Emergency Conference in 1944 included Spain among the countries which were thanked for "the protection they offered under difficult conditions to the persecuted Jews in Hungary,"[328] and one of the World Jewish Congress leaders, Isaac Weismann, paid a special tribute to the "chivalrous attitude and Christian sentiments" shown by the Franco government.[329] At the same time, it is worth noting that the Sephardic Jews so rescued were not encouraged to remain in the country which after all claimed to regard them as its own.

> [Spain's] recognition of her nationals was limited to recognition of them as individuals to be permitted transit through Spain, but not as nationals entitled to reside in Spain. . . . Spain's attitude revealed without a doubt that, in spite of the Sephardic Jews' common cultural heritage with Spain, the latter had no interest in absorbing them permanently, nor was she prepared to do so. The possibility that a large number of Jews might return to live in Spain on a permanent basis was the factor which deterred those who determined policy within the Spanish Foreign Office. . . . The "Spaniards without a Homeland" were condemned to go on living—or die—outside the "homeland".[330]

At the end of 1945, a mere 600 Jewish refugees were left in Spain, one half receiving assistance from the Intergovernmental Committee on Refugees, the other being aided by the JDC.[331]

Nor were conditions inside Spain calculated to make Jews feel welcome. The French Sephardim in 1943 found a less than encouraging reception:

> A kind of economic inquisition had been putting slow but strong pressure on them to abandon Judaism and to lose their identity completely, but even at the price of calculated total assimilation they were unable to exercise any trade other than that of peddler, and to avoid repeated nuisance sentences of short terms of imprisonment on flimsy pretexts. Of this group perhaps the majority desired to go to Palestine.[332]

Antisemitism was still strong, at least German influence saw to it that "in the press and in literature anti-Jewish sentiments are expressed,"[333] though the German ambassador in Madrid regretfully noted that "for the majority of the Spanish people and for the official ideology of the State no Jewish problem exists." In fact, occasionally the press would openly disapprove of German Jew-baiting. When the Yellow Badge was introduced in occupied France, the paper of the Falange, shunning the Nazi terminology of a "solution of the Jewish problem," frankly referred to "the persecution of a people"; antisemites must have been gnashing their teeth as they read here (of all places) the Balaam-like report: "When on the first day the Badge was noticed in the streets of Paris, it seemed as if these people not merely wore something that distinguished them, but rather as if a shining light went forth from them."[334]

Still, as late as October 1944, Radio Falange was able to broadcast such propaganda as this: "The Jewish danger is no unfounded fantasy. Bound up with Communism, passionately interested in the victory of the Communist ideology which denies Christ, Jewry makes every effort to create the appropriate situation for the fatal destruction of the Christian world. It is on account of all this that nothing is more urgent at the moment than to fight against the Communist and the Jew."[335]

In the same year, a professor Vicente Risco published a well-advertised "History of the Jews" which was little better than Radio Falange propaganda.[336] It quoted the "Protocols of Zion" as an unimpeachable authority and the tale of the Wandering Jew as authentic history.[337] The book was subjected to scathing criticism by one of Spain's foremost scholars, Professor Francisco Cantera Burgos, who confessed to "veritable feelings of pain and humiliation" at the sight of this "gross insult to Spain, calculated to lower her prestige."[338]

The criticism appeared in the journal of the government institute founded in 1940 to promote Arabic and Hebrew Studies—*Instituto Benito Arias Montano de Estudios Arabes y Hebraicos*. This Institute, under its directors Francisco Cantera Burgos and José M. Millás Vallicrosa, was dedicated to the study of "Hebrew-Biblical cultural problems" and the civilization of the ancient world in relation to the Hebrews: "We shall take pride in the knowledge that Spain now contributes her share to the great debate on the cultural relations between the Bible and the Semitic orbit of the Middle East—Egypt, Phoenicia, Babylon, Assyria, Iran." The Institute was also conceived to give attention to another subject: the Hebrew-Spanish tradition. The Institute's journal *Sefarad* explained: "Spanish Jewry, in the course of its residence in Spain, was moving almost entirely in spheres of the spirit. . . . It should be remembered that Spanish Judaism attained the highest achievements in the way of religious poetry, Bible exegesis, Hebrew philology, philosophy and science."[339]

Sympathy for and the ancient links with Jews found a practical expression soon after the war in the decree of 29 December 1948 confirming the Spanish nationality of certain Sephardic families which had enjoyed that privilege since the days of the Ottoman Empire.[340] No doubt this step was taken mainly to appease anti-Spanish feelings; also because the capitulations under the 1937 Convention of Montreux would be coming to an end in 1949, and it was considered imperative to reinforce the legal status of those who, "because of their love for our country," had for so long been protected by Spain. A semi-official commentary said:

> This decree constitutes one more proof of the lofty spirit which animates Spain in international affairs and which has no truck with any kind of racism. Ancient quarrels caused the departure of these Sephardic Jews from the soil of their ancestors, but Spain never ceased to hark to the voice of its own language which was perpetuated among these Sephardim, and Spain has repeatedly shown a lively interest in their fate.[341]

The decree was accompanied by a government memorandum entitled *El Sefardismo*.[342] It was circulated among Spanish consular agents abroad with a view to stressing the importance which the Franco regime proposed to attach to the existence of Sephardic communities in many parts of the world. The total number of Sephardim in and near Europe was then (before 1948) believed to be five hundred and fifty thousand with another two hundred and twenty-five thousand living in North and South America, in Central Africa and Indonesia.

Once again advantage was to be taken of the ancient Spanish-Jewish association for the furtherance of Spanish interests. Characteristically, the outstanding event in the history of Spanish Jews after 1492 was seen in the invitation extended to them by Sultan Bayacetus II to settle in his kingdom, with guarantees of individual and collective liberty. Ever since there had been Sephardic colonies in all large cities of the Ottoman Empire, and the Sephardim now enjoyed a considerable amount of freedom as the Turkish state practiced the policy of noninterference in the domestic and religious customs of its non-Turkish subjects so long as they were politically trustworthy. There could be no doubt that the Jews were among the Sultan's most loyal subjects and it was these Jews who were now said to have preserved in the most perfect manner their affinity with Spain.

The memorandum also referred to Zionism which it viewed with peculiarly ambivalent feelings. On the one hand, Zionism seemed "a danger to the continued existence of Sephardism" because "it is a barrier to the spreading of our culture and the preservation of our language and our customs among these Spaniards who have no country." Zionism was said to constitute "a national opposition to all the countries that have contributed throughout the centuries to the fulfillment of the Wandering Jew's destiny." (It is curious to note the strong hold which the story of the Wandering Jew has over Spanish minds). On the other hand, it was stated, Zionism should not be thought of as "synonymous with anti-Sephardism." Since the interest in Hebrew, for example, was "not political but purely cultural," Sephardism could "perfectly well accept the growing use of Spanish as an official language in their relations with western civilization," therefore it was "permitted to arrive at the conclusion that the Sephardim are part of a united effort for a national ideal, that the Sephardic views must inevitably be shared by the Spanish Jews, that they are in fact a second-degree Zionism to such an extent that the Spanish cannot be anti-Zionists but must necessarily be supporters and promoters of Zionism."

This was well said. Unfortunately the words were not followed by action that might have upheld the—particularly then—struggling cause of Zionism; certainly the State of Israel was not recognized. Thus, perhaps unavoidably, attention was chiefly fastened on the ulterior motives of the decree, particularly so among the Spanish critics of the regime. The one-time Foreign Minister of the Spanish Republic, J. Alvarez del Vayo, did not deny that Franco had made "an intelligent gesture" but then he must have been "desperately anxious" to "break down the barrier keeping Spain out of the United Nations"; accordingly he was "trying to make himself popular in the U.S.A.," and "knowing the great influence exercised by the Jewish community there, he made a gesture of propitiation." Actually, Alvarez del Vayo said, the Jews had been told they would have the same rights as Spain's twenty-five thousand Protestants, but what did that mean? The rights of Protestants under Franco were "practically nil." It was true

> on paper, perfect freedom of religion exists in Spain; it is guaranteed by the *Fuero de los Españoles* [Bill of Rights] promulgated in 1945 and by various solemn affirmations of Franco's. The most recent of these, made in 1947, declared that "no man shall be persecuted for his religious faith." Although the *Fuero de los Españoles* purports to protect the Rights of Man, in reality so far as religious freedom is concerned, it is pure rhetoric. Spain is the only country in Europe today where the Bible is forbidden literature. The few Protestant schools that still exist since Franco made education the exclusive monopoly of the religious orders carry on half illegally. They are not prohibited by any particular decree, but Protestant teachers seem fated to come into conflict with the law. They are always being accused of associating with subversive political elements. . . .[343]

More especially, Alvarez del Vayo pointed out, Protestant churches were not allowed to have any exterior identification; billboards were forbidden as proselytizing devices to attract new members. consequently, he thought, "the Sefardic Jews whom we Spanish republicans have always regarded as our compatriots, would do well to renounce with thanks the protection extended to them by Franco. They might better wait until liberty is again the law of the land, until Spain has a government which will be happy to have them participate in its efforts for recovery and peace." It was of course inevitable for Spain to emerge from the war with an image tragically tarnished through Franco's association, however ambiguous, with Hitler. In the heat even after the battle her good deeds were ignored and antisemitism seemed to be written all over her. A penetrating symptom of it was revealed on a relatively trivial occasion.

When in 1948 the Spanish government banned the American film *Gentlemen's Agreement* which exposed the evil of antisemitism, the Church censor argued that since Christians and Jews were portrayed as equals here, a dangerous poison was spread; Jews were being encouraged to feel pride which they had no business to feel since they were as "perfidious as they were called in the holy scriptures"; it was no Christian's duty to stimulate love for the Jews, because they were enemies of the Church.[344] The government Chief Film Censor, Garcia Espina, sought to mitigate these (even to him) embarrassing strictures. There was no antisemitism in Spain, he insisted, but the film would tend to raise bias where it did not exist. "In Spain we don't know of the conflict between Semitism and Antisemitism. The anguish of racial differences which disturbs the lives of other people is alien to us and we want it to continue being alien."[345] And so there was no *Gentlemen's Agreement*.

Shortly after, as if trying to redress the balance, the government gave permission to reopen the synagogue in Madrid. It was consecrated on 2 January 1949, in a sub-basement of Cardenal Cisneros, 62; its rabbi was José Cuby, and its lay leaders were Ignacio Bauer, Daniel Navon, a prominent business-

man, and Moisés Lawanda, a Polish Jew.[346] Later, in 1958, the synagogue
moved to a second-floor "Beth Sion" at Calle Pizarro, 19. In 1954, two
synagogues—one Sephardic and one Ashkenazic—were opened in Barcelona.[347]
Services however were to be strictly private. The Primate of Spain, Cardinal Pla y
Daniel, emphasized this point: both Jews and Protestants were free to practice
their religion in private; this right was embodied in the Bill of Rights, granted
as "a kind of friendly action towards foreigners living in Spain." Public
observance, the cardinal explained, was forbidden because of "the danger that
some political minority might take advantage of the ceremonies to disseminate
their progaganda."[348]

These views met with severe criticism in the *Jewish Chronicle*. Clearly, it
was said, Spain knew as yet "no true religious freedom"; not even Soviet
Russia imposed such restrictions on religious practice. Was it seriously suggested
that the few Jews congregating in Madrid were likely to endanger the Franco
regime? If so, it was "a confession of both arbitrariness and weakness."[349]

Spain and Israel

Feeling toward Spain was certainly not mollified by such incidents, and it
was therefore not surprising perhaps when one of the first actions of the new State
of Israel as a member of the United Nations was to vote against the proposed
lifting of the United Nations diplomatic embargo on Franco Spain; the
reason given was not that the Spanish regime was undemocratic but that Spain
had been an ally of the Nazis;[350] the "link to the Nazi-fascist alliance" still
seemed too glaring.[351] Franco was annoyed; he had not expected this because
he thought that Israel had understood the circumstances of his association
with Hitler.[352] A year later, in October 1950, Israel once more supported an
anti-Spanish move, refusing to revoke the original United Nations recommen-
dation; but now she was in a minority, and generally, too, feelings began to
relent.

Jewry's intellectual and spiritual association with Spain was strikingly demonstrated in October 1952 by the Israeli delegate to the United Nations,
Moshe Tov, when he supported the adoption of Spanish as one of the official
languages of the United Nations Economic and Social Council.[353] It is true he
concentrated on Latin America and on practical rather than sentimental
considerations, but even so, he could not help dwelling on the Sephardim's
"love for and identification with Spain" which had "shown itself in the last
four centuries." After all, they had been in that land before the language was
born, in Phoenician and Carthaginian times. They had taken "the treasure
of the language" with them into exile, had handed it down from father to
son wherever they might have been—in Buenos Aires, Montevideo, Quito, in
Salonika or Manhattan—and in 1935, at the time of the Maimonides celebra-
tions, the Israeli delegate recalled, the Spanish Republic had made a "grand

historic reparation" by "restoring the firm direct bonds which link the
Sephardic communities all over the world with the linguistic cradle of all the
peoples of Spain."

Time seemed to carry healing in its wings. Spain was clearly changing.
A notable schism began to develop between government and the Church.[354]
Franco himself made the most of the denominations' private rights under the
Spanish charter.[355] In 1953 he received the President of the Madrid Jewish
community, Daniel Francois Baroukh, and the government was represented at
a Rosh Hashanah service in the capital.[356] Growing interest in Spain's relations
with the United States made it seem desirable to reassure the American
public, and so, in a special interview with a widely read American magazine,
Franco stressed not only the existence of several synagogues in the country but
also the absence of any "discrimination against Jewish businessmen." In fact,
he said, there had never been any antisemitism in Spain, on the contrary,
"The Jews have been able to develop themselves perfectly in our nation."[357]

"Perfectly" was perhaps a less than perfect description, but there were
welcome developments. At the great World Sephardic Bibliographical Exhibi-
tion in Madrid in 1959, it was announced that the Spanish Academy would
form a special section to study Sephardic culture and the Ladino language,[358]
and in 1961 an Institute of Sephardic Studies was indeed established.[359]
Spain's concern with the Sephardim was eloquently avowed at the solemn
occasion when the monument of Maimonides was unveiled in Córdoba in
June 1964. Spain, said the civil governor of the city, was "a country at peace
for all Spaniards and those who feel themselves Spaniards through the bonds of
the blood, of the race and language," and this included "you Sephardim
bound as you are by your past to an Iberian ancestral home where you
find all that ever was yours, all that still is yours, all that, by the will of
the Spanish government, continues to constitute part of the spiritual and
cultural heritage of a community which has maintained alive, in its purest
kind, our Castillian tongue of the fifteenth century."[360]

By now too the Vatican Council made its influence felt. In fact as early
as 1962 Jews and Christians began to consider the advantages of cooperation.
A meeting was held in Madrid, presided over by Dr. Cantero Burgos,
professor of Hebrew, and addressed by a representative of the Archbishop of
Madrid, Fr. Vicente Serrano, and the Haham of the British Sephardim, Dr.
Solomon Gaon. "Only cooperation between our religions can save us," said
Dr. Gaon: "It is necessary to fight against materialism with the arms of our
spiritual values."[361]

A German observer commended the Church for the tolerance shown the
Jews which he said was greater than that displayed toward Protestants.[362] This
attitude would change, he thought, as soon as the Jews claimed equal status
as a religious community, and Dr. Gaon's remarks met in fact with some
reserve. The widely read Catholic daily *Ya* warned against "excessive" tolerance

toward Jews on the ground that the Israelis were discriminating against con-
verted Jews, and in the Falange paper, *Arriba,* a priest, Fr. Ricart Torreas,
while admitting that antisemitism was condemned by the Church, categorically,
"refused to fall into the extreme of philosemitism which is, in political terms,
Liberalism."

Under the impact of the Vatican Council, however, the cause of reconciliation prospered. A Jewish-Christian Friendship Association (*Amistad*) arose,[363]
and under its auspices, a group of priests of Madrid's Santa Rita Church and
leaders of the Jewish community arranged a joint service in the church, an event
without precedent in Spain.[364] Prayers were chosen that were common to both
religions, such as Psalm 126 whose text, "When the Lord turned again the
captivity of Zion, then were we like unto them that dream" was thought to be
particularly appropriate for Spaniards separated so long.

The Polish-born president of the Jewish community, Max Mazin, praised
Pope John XXIII saying that he would go down in history as a "good and
generous Pope, inspired and providential"; thanks to him, "we are united here
and later will be in our synagogue. All that we have in common is much
more important and more transcendental than what separates us." Fr. Jesús
Alvarez also emphasized the common interests that exist between Catholics
and Jews in the light of the Vatican Council and said that they must learn
to live together. A prayer for peace was sung in Hebrew, and the reunion
ended with the chanting of Psalm 136. The harmony now extended sufficiently far for Catholics to urge recognition of the State of Israel. The daily
Ya felt it was an anomaly that Spain, eighteen years after the creation of the
Jewish state, was the only nation in western Europe that did not recognize it.
The paper noted particularly that "this disconcerts our many friends in America
and Europe."[365]

For many Spanish Roman Catholics, however, the emergence of the State
of Israel presented baffling questions, and faint rumblings of the old theological
antisemitism could still be heard. The Archbishop of Madrid, Cardinal
Tarancón, no doubt had them in mind when in September 1972 he established
a diocesan Christian-Jewish Study Center designed to "enlighten Christians on
the roots of their own faith through knowledge of Judaism in whose bosom
Christianity was born."[366] Equally, since 1974, Christian-Jewish harmony has
been promoted by a Spanish-Israel Seminar meeting once a year,[367] and an
Association for Judeo-Christian Relations is concerning itself especially with
the very necessary survey of school textbooks. Cardinal Tarancón also took
notable action when he declared membership of extreme Right-wing parties
to be incompatible with the Christian faith; totalitarian regimes and acts of
violence were inhuman and therefore un-Christian.[368]

In the meantime, the Jews had begun to extend their communal organization. An unofficial Council of Jewish Communities in Spain, comprising
Madrid, Ceuta and Melilla, was formed in the spring of 1964,[369] and in March

1965, two months after the heads of the Madrid and Barcelona congregations had been received by General Franco,[370] legal status was granted to a Madrid Council, though not as a public but merely as a strictly private association. This was the only non-Catholic religious association with juridical status. At the same time the community was asked to change its name from "La Communidad Israelita de Madrid" to "La Communidad Hebrea de Madrid" to avoid confusion with the State of Israel.[371]

From the rule to recognize only "local" associations, an exception was made in the case of the *Asociación Hebrea de España* which was recognized in 1972 as being national in scope. Its declared purpose was similar to that of Jewish defense agencies in other countries, as contrasted with strictly religious Jewish activity: to strengthen the image of Judaism and promote Christian-Jewish amity. The *Asociación* was formed by Max Mazin after a long-drawn-out internal controversy concerned with the degree of Christian-Jewish involvement and the centralization of communal authority. In February 1970, Mazin decided to resign from the Madrid leadership, leaving the field to various factions which did not arrive at a compromise until April 1973.

This unedifying spectacle occurred during a period of crucial decisions for the cause of religious liberty. In 1967 the much debated and long delayed law on religious freedom came into force (Law 44/1967, dated 28 June 1967). It was intended to mark the transition from a regime of tolerance, with its privileges for the Roman Catholic Church, to a regime of religious liberty in which the state guarantees the enjoyment of liberty to all religious communities in Spain. The law recognized "religious liberty as a fundamental right of the dignity of the human person."

> It guaranteed also the public profession and practice of religion and a variety of individual rights flowing from this, e.g. equal facilities for marriage and burial for non-Catholics as for Catholics; the right to choose the faith of one's children. It also enabled "all non-Catholic religious confessions (to) apply for legal recognition by constituting religious associations," to be governed by their own statutes and to "obtain juridical personality in all respects once inscribed in a special Government register provided for by the law." Before this, only Madrid's Jewish community had officially recognized status, and only as a private association.[372]

The provision that "non-Catholic associations" had to submit to a degree of governmental control by securing "registration" aroused some criticism. Strong disagreement was expressed by Mazin.[373] He took exception to the "legal shackles" that were being proposed. He said that they were all very well in the case of a bullfighters' club or a business corporation, but a religious community should not be subject to legal control; religious liberty was an "objective right given by God to all men" and did not depend on any sponsor in Parliament whatever his religion. As it was, equality of rights for all Spaniards in religious matters had definitely not been achieved; the law did not conform

to the principles of religious liberty proclaimed by the Vatican Council.
Even so, Mazin thought, an "enormous step forward" had been made; the
Spanish people had accepted religious liberty as something completely normal.
An association like *Amistad,* for example, had been totally inconceivable as
recently as the 1950s: "This greatly assures us, even though the legal device
does not satisfy us."

Now the stage was set for the most memorable event in modern Spanish-
Jewish history: the opening of an officially sanctioned synagogue, the first since
1350.[374] On 14 December 1968 the government issued a statement in which
(a) the Hebrew Congregation of Madrid was expressly recognized and "full
rights of citizenship" were conferred on "the Jewish religion," and (b) for the
first time ever the edict of expulsion was specifically revoked. Two days later,
on 16 December, the second day of Hanukkah (26 Kislev 5729), the "Beth
Yaacov" in Balmes, 3, was consecrated in the presence of a large congregation
which included, among Jews, representatives from all over Spain and Morocco,
the United States, Britain, Portugal, and Argentina; also with representatives of
international Jewish organizations such as the JDC, the World Jewish Congress,
the World Sephardic Federation, the European Council of Jewish Communities,
and among Christians not only representatives of various churches in Spain
but also the director general of the Spanish Foreign Office, the secretary general
of the Ministry of Information and Tourism, the secretary of the Interminis-
terial Commission on Religious Liberty, the acting mayor of Madrid and a
representative of the director general of the Press.

The "historic event" was interpreted by Mazin in the sense that "a grave
injustice committed against our people nearly five hundred years ago is now
finding its legal redress in accordance with the new times in which we live."
Leaving aside the all too obvious "painful memories," he spoke of the "hopeful
future for a life side by side, in dignity and mutual respect, among the children
of God," a "new era for all men of good will." There was curiously little
comment in the general press. An article in the evening paper *El Pueblo* re-
flected on "the change that has come about in the country's mentality as
shown in the new law on religious liberty."[375] Many Spaniards were "redis-
covering their Jewish-Christian past," realizing how much both had in common.
The "Spanish synagogue" would help establish important links between Christians
and Jews, for too often the tragedy of the past has been caused by "mutual
ignorance and barren suspicion."

How much ignorance and suspicion existed was revealed in two studies of
Spanish Jewry which now emerged—one a very substantial, scholarly effort,
the massive three volumes of Julio Caro Baroja, *Los Judíos en la España
moderna y contemporánea* (Madrid, 1961-62); the other *Los Judios españoles,*
by Felipe Torroba Bernaldo de Quirós (Madrid, 1967). The title of the first
is somewhat misleading since the subject is not only modern and contemporary
but medieval Spain as well. In fact, the author, a trained historian who had

published extensively on various aspects of Spanish history including crypto-Judaism and the Moorish period, set out to trace the story of "the opposition of Judaism and Christianity as representative religions of two societies," with "the conflict between men and powers as proof of the existence of something like a blind fate and not as a theme of national or cultural history" (vol. I, p. 15).

Caro Baroja explains his position as follows: "I am not singing the praises of what happened in Spain between the end of the fifteenth and the end of the seventeenth centuries. On the other hand, so far as the Jews are concerned, I am not one of those philosemites who treat everything to do with Jews uncritically. I am revolted by the excesses of Nazi racialism. I admire many figures of the Jewish world. But I have no sufficient reason either to sympathize with or to hate the heads of the ghetto. That's all. Jews and Christians, as groups, cannot always be either good or bad, among them will inevitably be found the dubious characters that exist in every people. Why make history a register in which evil and goodness will always be entered in the same places?" (vol. I, p. 16).

By contrast, Torroba's book is literally a lightweight. It had actually appeared in 1958, as a third of its present size, and was then, written in English, little more than an essay in public relations clearly for the benefit of Anglo-Saxon tourists. Now a Spanish as well as an English edition was printed. The otherwise unknown author who appears to have been influenced by Vicente Risco is a product of pre-conciliar "Christian" teaching. The "terrible curse pronounced on Ahasuerus," repeatedly mentioned (pp. 6, 292), is treated as a legitimate feature of history; pogroms are presented as "a weapon of social purification" (p. 6), and the expulsion is justified as "the only way to put an end to the 'Jewish menace' " — "a cyst in the body of the nation" (the English version adds, p. 277) — the previous killings having "proved that it was not possible to 'drown the Israelites in blood' " (p. 277). Now, it is said, Spain has "forgotten the old quarrels" (p. 356), and stress is laid on the material harm believed to have been suffered by the country as a result of the expulsion.

Spanish Historians' View of the Expulsion

These themes appear in many variations among Spanish historians, some rebuking their country, some passionately defending it. Characteristically in the Second Republic, a severe view is taken. Ulloa denounces the "brutal" expulsion which he says was "flying in the face of the relative toleration practiced until then," though he finds it was also supported by "the fanaticism of the masses" and "a logical sequel to the establishment of the Inquisition." He points out that while Jews were allowed to sell their property "freely," they were nevertheless forbidden to take any of the proceeds out of the country. The "compulsory sale" at 5 per cent of the true value was in fact "a confiscation," so that "many Christians grew rich on this occasion." Emphasis is laid on the "affection" with which the Sephardim, repaying evil with good, even now remember their ancient homeland.[376]

The early stages of the Franco regime reveal the influence of Nazi propaganda. Giménez has no good word for the Jewish "aliens" who by "exploiting" the people had "aroused hatred against themselves," "corrupted" the "ideas of religion, fatherland and nation," had "fomented social discord" and had given rise to fears (shades of the "Protocols of Zion"!) that "through their international connections," they were "seeking to control the government." Spaniards and Jews are found to have been "mutually repellent," and a summary charge accused the "insincere converts" of "replacing spiritualism by materialism."[377]

In a similar vein, Silió tries to justify the expulsion as "necessary" because otherwise the Jews "would have become the first financial power of the world."[378] He canvasses the ancient tale of the "people without a fatherland and condemned never to have one," as "wanderers over the face of the earth without finding their own land," who are "incapable of the two qualities which maintain a fatherland"—physical labor and military prowess. The Jesuit Cereda stresses the "social and religious threat" which the Jews are said to have fostered: the Spanish people had been "economically oppressed" and "mocked in the most intimate of their religious feelings."[379]

Perhaps the most virulent reviler of the Jews, however, is another priest, Fernández de Retana, a Redemptorist, who compiled a veritable catalogue of almost every argument likely to vindicate the expulsion—an event "made irresistible by the unanimous will of the people." He sees Spaniards and Jews locked in a "fight to the death" and "irreconcilable hate" since the very earliest times. Any suggestion expecting toleration in those days is dismissed as a plea for "miserable indifference to an unconcern with the paramount purpose of man." Besides, this writer asks, what sort of tolerance did the Jews find outside Spain? The expulsions from England and France are cited; even Martin Luther the antisemite finds favor in the eyes of the diehard Roman Catholic. Altogether no one can blame Spain now considering that "today we have seen the most advanced modern states expelling their Jews as undesirables."[380]

The comparison between "the exclusively religious measure" in 1492 and the "racialist persecutions in Europe today" also provides a crumb of comfort for a more moderate historian, Jiménez, who regards what he calls the "departure" from Spain as "the only solution to the fundamental differences separating Christians and Jews." He notes the Jews' "love of Spain" which they were "demonstrating by the sorrow over the new Babylonian captivity." While Fernández is not quite sure how to answer "the eternal question of the economic advantages of the expulsion," Jiménez has no doubt that "our society was deprived of its only specialists in commerce."[381]

A very different verdict is passed by another scholar of the Franco era. Ballesteros is impressed by the manifestation of "a great idea"—Spain's religious unity—and this, to him, makes all the difference when comparing the expulsion with "the medieval pogroms and the contemporary killings" which were "motivated by racial or social enmity." Moreover, he says, the expulsion was "good for the Jews themselves," because their lives were "gravely threatened by their own foolishness and the hatred of the Christians." He writes: "From this point of view, the antisemitic solution appears as the most humane ever applied in history."[382]

In order to arrive at this conclusion, Ballesteros has to rake up most of the time-dishonored calumnies, not excluding the "ritual murder" lie and the charge of a "cosmopolitan internationalism" which "maintained relations with the enemies of Spain."[383] On the other hand, he for one cannot deny that at least Queen Isabel "was well aware of all the signal services the Jews had rendered to the Crown"; in fact she "loved them as her loyal subjects," but what could she do against "the paramount popular feeling"?

A more sophisticated defense of the expulsion is undertaken by Armiñan. He calls in the perspective of history. Consider the spirit of the age, he argues: "The heretic's life counted for little, as indeed anybody's life. To live for God and to die for Him: everything else was of no consequence." The expulsion is seen as the reflection of a nationalist and religious sentiment not peculiar to the fifteenth century. Religious persecution is deemed something that is always with us, and the charges levelled against the Jews in every generation appear so identical that "the monotony of history is really astonishing." Besides, Armiñan, like Jiménez, draws comfort from the relativity of inhumanity: "To let a people emigrate is certainly less cruel than to kill it in the horrors of the concentration camps."[384]

According to Armiñan, there were many Christians feeling pity for the persecuted Jews whose chief offense, it is plainly intimated, was not religious non-conformity but rather their industry, genius and success and whose undoing their "trust in vain hopes." Armiñan himself pays a notable tribute to Jewry: "No race [he writes] has shown greater ability to resist the most cruel persecutions and to survive them. . . . Many empires, and of course individuals and whole generations, which attempted to exterminate the Jews, have passed away while they went on. . . . In its spirit the race brought forth a second nature which was the force that saved it." In the ebb and flow of this debate, attempts were now made, under government auspices, to remove the vestiges of the past. Some of the synagogues which had been abandoned or put to other use during the centuries were rebuilt or restored. Often they were in places without a Jewish congregation; the idea was to preserve the buildings as historical monuments.[385] The ancient *El Tránsito* synagogue in Toledo had already been so restored during the reign of Alfonso XIII who in fact showed a personal interest in it,[386] and now it was opened as a Sephardic museum.[387]

The centuries since the expulsion came at last full circle—almost exactly a hundred years after the memorable constitution—on 28 May 1976 when the queen of Spain, the successor of Isabella, attended a Sabbath eve service in the new Madrid synagogue.[388] Queen Sophie who was received by Rabbi Benito Garzón and the President of the *Kehillah*, Felipe Halioua, was accompanied by the Auxiliary Bishop of Madrid (representing Cardinal Tarancón) and leaders of the Spanish Reformed, Baptist, Lutheran and Mormon churches, as well as by the undersecretary of the Ministry of Justice. Her visit was presented as part of the normal cultural activities of Madrid University's Department of Contemporary Humanities where the queen is studying the religions of the world including Judaism.

In a speech at a dinner subsequently given in her honor, Queen Sophie spoke of the "new and enriching experience" which the study of Judaism was giving to all taking part in it:

> The Second Vatican Council and the law on Religious Liberty in Spain inspire us to engage in a fraternal dialogue and to respect for all religions, Christian and non-Christian, including Judaism, because of its significance in the beginnings of our faith and in the spiritual grandeur in which Christians and Jews share. The activities of the Department of Humanities and the dialogue which we have fostered in the Seminar on Judaism, as in other seminars, are a token of the vision which we all cherish of a Spain enjoying harmony and unity.

A short time after, in December 1976, a notable gesture of goodwill was made by the World Jewish Congress which decided to hold a meeting of its European branch in Madrid. The decision was taken at the request of Spanish Jewry who in turn had obtained their government's agreement.[389] The purpose of the meeting was twofold: (1) "to show that attitudes toward Jews had changed"; and (2) to give "changing Spain political support."[390] The World Jewish Congress believed that "such a meeting would be in the interests of the community, that it would serve as a source of inspiration to its members and foster their sense of solidarity with fellow-Jews throughout the world, and that it would enhance the position and status of Spanish Jewry in the eyes of their countrymen."[391]

The occasion was appropriately considered a milestone in history.[392] Dr. Nahum Goldmann, president of the World Jewish Congress, spoke of "a very important political and historical event, marking the reconciliation between Spain and the Jews."[393] He added gratuitously, "To punish Spain for the expulsion of the Jews in 1492, the rabbis have for centuries forbidden any Jews to visit the country."[394] He paid a special tribute to Franco: "We have no complaint against him" as he had always adopted a fair attitude toward the Jews, never shown himself in favor of the Nuremberg Laws, saved the lives of hundreds of Jews by refusing to hand them over to the Germans and allowed them to live in Spain.[395] Lord Fisher of Camden, chairman of the World Jewish Congress European branch, thought the Jews had now "officially returned to Spain,"[396] and in the Madrid press the meeting was hailed as "proof of the total change on the part of the international Jewish community"[397] and as an "historical reparation" for the expulsion in 1492.[398] Accordingly a warm welcome was extended to the Jews on behalf of the city of Madrid by its mayor, Don Juan de Arespacochaga, who dwelt on the Jewish contribution to the culture of Spain.[399]

In this atmosphere an occasion of some significance also was the laying of the cornerstone of the first officially recognized Jewish school in Madrid since the Inquisition. The ceremony was attended by representatives of the Ministry of Education.[400] The school, named the *Colegio Judío Ibn Gabirol,* which can accommodate four hundred pupils was opened a year later.[401] However, in the larger field of Spanish-Jewish relations, the government kept strangely aloof. The deputy minister of justice was to have welcomed the conference and a Jewish delegation was to have been received by the king. Suddenly the minister excused himself and the Jews agreed to withdraw their request for an audience. The mystery was quickly resolved. News of the conference had reached the Arab envoys who promptly expressed their displeasure in terms that left no doubt about its unfortunate practical effect on Spanish-Arab relations. In fact "diplomatic pressure"[402] was exerted to prevent what (it was felt) "could be the start of Spain's recognition of Israel."[403]

The fears were wholly unfounded. The conference took great pains to confine its concern to Spanish-Jewish business. Dr. Goldmann stressed that "under no circumstances would the World Jewish Congress use the Madrid meeting for the purpose of acting as an intermediary in the normalization of relations between Spain and Israel."[404] At the same time, it could not be denied that "any issue to do with the Jews is a touchy one for the Spanish Government," and there were reasons, for example, to sustain the widespread belief that the Governor of the Bank of Spain, Señor Luis Coronel de Palma, had recently been dismissed because of his remark that Spain and Israel would soon extend diplomatic recognition to each other.[405] Spain relies on Arab investment and it so happened she was just negotiating a two billion dollar loan from Saudi Arabia.[406]

Under the circumstances, it was probably not unwarranted to suspect a "surrender to Arab blackmail,"[407] though such surrender could hardly be said to "illustrate the struggle between the old and new traditions within Spain itself."[408] Nor was it perhaps fair or accurate for the paper of Israel's National Religious party, *Ha-tsofeh,* to describe the surrender as "neither anti-Zionist nor anti-Israel but antisemitic pure and simple."[409] The massive protest was not anticipated but it could not have come entirely as a surprise, except to those who believe that Arab "anti-Zionists" could never be anti-Jewish. Dr. Goldmann clarified the position:

> When the Jewish Community of Spain invited the European branch of the World Jewish Congress to meet in Madrid — a fact which was widely publicised throughout the world — the Spanish Government agreed to welcome the delegates and the King expressed his willingness to receive a deputation. Under these circumstances there was every reason to assume

that the holding of the meeting in Madrid would be helpful in the progress of normalizing relations between Spain and the Jewish people, and thereby the State of Israel.

Dr. Goldmann also referred to the "apparent" impact of "Arab pressure."

The World Jewish Congress keenly regretted the unhappy turn of events. The Spanish authorities, they said, preferred to consider the Jewish meeting in the context of "day-to-day Spanish-Arab relations" rather than "in the historic context of re-establishing relations between the Jewish people and the new Spain" after almost five hundred years.[410] The Israelis were angry. Moshe Dayan felt that the Jews had received "a slap in the face."[411] The way Spain behaved toward Israel was an "insult to the Jewish people as a whole," for "what kind of 'reconciliation' is it so long as Spain refuses to recognize the State of Israel?" In retrospect, Dayan thought, "it was a good thing that the reconciliation bid came to nothing."

Spain is indeed adamant in her refusal to recognize Israel. In November 1976 she voted at the United Nations in favor of a Palestinian state,[412] and the Spanish Foreign Minister, Señor Marcelino Oreja Aguirre, repeatedly called for "due satisfaction to be given to the just demands of the Arab nations."[413] Solemn affirmations of Spain's "traditional friendship" with the Arabs were designed to encourage the wealthy Arab nations to show greater interest in Spanish imports and Spanish technology.[414] On the other hand, strong forces are in favor of diplomatic relations. The Liberals were highly critical of Spain's United Nations vote,[415] and the Secretary of the Socialist Party, Señor Filipe Gonzales, on a visit to Tel Aviv, promised that relations would be established by a socialist government.[416] This remains to be seen. Yet, when that day comes and Spain does recognize Israel—not only so many individuals, not only the people of the Jews but also the state and government of the Jews—then perhaps it may be said that the last has been heard of the Ghosts of 1492.

NOTES

1. Caesar C. Aronsfeld, "The Cherem that never was," *Jewish Frontier* (July–August 1968), 27–28. Also, Tovia Preschel, "Did the Jews proclaim a Herem on Spain?" *The Alliance Review*, 24, 44 (Spring 1971), 18–19.

2. George Borrow, *The Bible in Spain* (London, 1961), p. 165. It was originally published in 1843.

3. José Amador de los Rios, *Historia Social, Política y Religiosa de los Judíos de España y Portugal* (Madrid, 1876), III, 548.

4. See Henry Charles Lea, *A History of the Inquisition in Spain* (New York, 1907), III, 313.

5. Amador, *Historia*, p. 552; also Lea, *ibid.*, p. 314.

6. Amador, *Historia*, p. 553.

7. Amador, *ibid.*

8. Lea, *History of the Inquisition*, pp. 314–15.

9. Borrow, *Bible in Spain*, p. 110.

10. Amador, *Historia*, pp. 555–56.

11. Lea, *History of the Inquisition* (New York, 1922), IV, 467 ff.

12. William C. Atkinson, *The History of Spain and Portugal* (London, 1960, reprinted 1967), p. 290. See also Raymond Carr, *Spain 1808–1939* in the *Oxford History of Modern Europe* (Oxford, 1966), p. 345. According to Julio Caro Baroja, *Los Judíos en la España Moderna y Contemporánea* (Madrid, 1962), III, 183, the caricaturists of the time were in the habit of depicting him with "an immense tail," for, says Felipe Torroba Bernaldo de Quirós, who draws heavily on Caro Baroja in his book, *Los Judíos Españoles* (Madrid, 1967), p. 307, "the idea that Jews have tails was still current."

13. Borrow, *Bible in Spain*, p. 343.

14. *Historia de los Judíos en España* (Cadiz, 1847), p. 7.

15. *The History of the Jews in Spain*, trans. by the Rev. Edward D. G. M. Kirwan, M.A. (Cambridge, 1851), p. 176.

16. *Ibid.*, pp. 3; 139–40; 141 and v–vi.

17. Amador, *Historia*, p. 570.

18. José Amador de los Rios, *Estudios históricos, políticos y literarios sobre los Judíos de España* (Buenos Aires, 1942), pp. 612; 609–16. It was originally published in Madrid, 1848.

19. Amador, *Historia*, p. 559.

20. *Allgemeine Zeitung des Judenthums*, 18 March 1850, p. 158, hereafter quoted as *AZJ*. The prohibition was of course frequently broken. In 1851, two German Jews were expelled from Madrid. See *AZJ*, 20 October 1851, p. 512.

21. Atkinson, *History of Spain and Portugal*, p. 282.

22. *Ibid.*, p. 285.

23. See Charles H. L. Emanuel, *A Century and a Half of Jewish History. Extracted from the Minute Book of the London Committee of Deputies of the British Jews* (London, 1910), p. 66.

24. *AZJ*, 28 August 1854, p. 437.

25. *Ibid.*, 25 September 1854, pp. 490–94.

26. *Ibid.*, pp. 489–90. In its reply, the *Consistoire* of Bayonne urged combined representative action by the Jews of France, Germany and Britain, but (they said) should Dr. Philippson prefer his "isolated" approach, they would be willing to assist through the good offices of "honorable personages in Madrid." See Henry Léon, *Histoire des Juifs de Bayonne* (Paris, 1893), pp. 352–53.

27. As quoted in *AZJ*, 4 December 1854, p. 617.

28. From the proclamation of the revolutionary *junta* at Irún, quoted in *AZJ*, 25 September 1854, p. 489.

29. *The Jewish Chronicle*, London, 20 November 1868, p. 5, hereafter quoted as *JC*.

30. Atkinson, *History of Spain and Portugal*, p. 286.

31. Carr, *Spain 1808-1939*, p. 285.

32. *AZJ*, 20 October 1868, p. 852, and *JC*, 20 November 1868, p. 5.

33. Léon, *Histoire des Juifs*, p. 354.

34. Amador, *Historia*, p. 561.

35. Paris correspondent of the London *Times*, 10 October 1862, quoted in *JC*, 17 October 1862, p. 6.

36. *AZJ*, 9 August 1864, p. 518.

37. *JC*, 10 February 1860, p. 5.

38. *JC*, 8 January 1864, p. 6, quoting the *Gibraltar Chronicle* 28 December 1863.

39. *JC*, 15 January 1864, p. 4.

40. The queen received Montefiore upon his return and congratulated him on his success. See Lucien Wolf, *Sir Moses Montefiore* (London, 1884), p. 231.

41. *JC*, 12 February 1864, p. 4.

42. Striking instances are given by Léon, *Histoire des Juifs*, p. 354, and Maxa Nordau, "Max Nordau en Espagne," *Le Judaisme Sephardi*, n.s., 31 (January 1966), 17.

43. *JC*, 19 February 1864, p. 5.

44. Angel Pulido Fernández, *Españoles sin Patria y la Raza Sefardí* (Madrid, 1905), p. 345.

45. Reporting this, the *JC*, 22 January 1867, p. 7, quotes the following statement by the Spanish foreign minister to the French minister of worship who had been approached by the French Jews: "If the French Israelites residing in this Kingdom wish to possess or purchase a piece of ground to bury their dead and wall it in, without erecting either a chapel or any kind of temple, without either a public or private worship, there exists no obstacle to give authority for such a structure, provided the said Israelites will undertake it at an opportune moment, conforming to the regulations of the Royal Ordinance of 13 November 1831, in virtue of which an analogous authorisation was given to the English Protestants, and in accordance with the law of 29 August 1855 which permits the establishment of cemeteries for the interment of the bodies of those who died outside the pale of the Catholic religion." See also the *Bulletin de l'Alliance Israélite Universelle*, Paris (April 1887), quoted in *AZJ*, 19 May 1887, p. 308.

46. *JC*, 19 February 1864, p. 5.

47. Paris correspondent of the London *Times*, quoted in *JC*, 6 November 1868, p. 8. This important episode in the history of the struggle for religious freedom in Spain, including the readmission of the Jews to that country has been treated by Joseph Lichtenstein, "Efforts to Re-establish a Jewish Community in Spain in the Mid-Nineteenth Century" (Hebrew), *Bar-Ilan Annual*, 7-8, (1970), 280-307. (The title of the article is more correctly translated from the Hebrew text as: Jewish efforts to achieve the abrogation of the Decree of Expulsion and Equality of Rights for their coreligionists in Spain in the Year 1868). While in many respects the author partly covers the same ground presented in this essay, he mentions a few details, largely derived from the Archives of the Department of State in Washington, D.C., some of which will be mentioned below. See Notes 54 and 59.

48. Léon, *Histoire des Juifs*, p. 358.

49. *JC*, 6 November 1868, p. 8, quoting the *Gibraltar Chronicle*.

50. *JC*, 20 November 1868, p. 5.

51. See the letter dated 20 October 1868 and addressed to a nephew of Sir Moses Montefiore, Haim Guedalla, a British champion of the Jews' right to settle in Spain, printed in *JC*, 13 November 1868, p. 7.

52. *JC*, 27 November 1868, p. 4.

53. *JC*, 8 January 1869, p. 7, and Amador, *Historia,* p. 562.

54. Emanuel, *Century and a Half,* p. 88. On Montefiore's intervention through Daniel Weisweiller, an agent of the House of Rothschild in Madrid, and Sir Moses' vain effort to involve the British government to intercede on behalf of the Board's petition, see Lichtenstein, "Efforts," pp. 283 f. and Notes 12-13.

55. 2 November 1868, quoted in *JC*, 13 November 1868, p. 6.

56. *JC*, 13 November 1868, p. 4.

57. Dated 4 December 1868, quoted in *JC*, 8 January 1869, p. 7.

58. In its magazine *Archives Israélites,* quoted in *JC, ibid.*

59. *AZJ*, 20 April 1869, p. 317, quoting a Madrid report in the *Neue Freie Presse,* Vienna. The reactionaries were aided by such excesses of the radical parties as the assassination of the governor of Burgos and the burning of a copy of the Papal Spanish Concordat in front of the Palace of the Papal Ambassador and the demonstrator's exclamation, "Long live liberated Rome!" See the dispatch of John Parker Hale dated 29 January 1869, no. 159, as quoted by Lichtenstein, "Efforts," pp. 289 f.

60. *JC*, 25 December 1868, p. 6.

61. *JC*, 23 April 1869, p. 10. See also Pulido, *Españoles sin Patria,* pp. 5 and 596-602. The speech created a profound impression at the time, if only perhaps as a feat of oratory. Pulido speaks of "the memorable sitting of 12 April" when "the Spanish tongue formed the most eloquent and moving invocation of religious tolerance ever heard in any Parliament of the world" (p. 5). In its obituary, the *JC*, 2 June 1899, p. 18, paid tribute to the "honey-tongued champion of toleration . . . inspired by a passionate love of liberty . . . the chivalrous Spaniard who over and over again lifted up his voice on behalf of the martyr-race of the world." See also Conde de Romanones, *Los Cuatro Presidentes de la Primera República Española* (n.p., 1939), pp. 117-61.

62. It is interesting to compare this state of mind with the reaction in 1943 of Mgr. Angelo Roncalli (later Pope John XXIII) to the idea of a Jewish commonwealth as the "realization of the messianic dream" which he was not prepared to further, though he was "quite certain that the restoration of the Kingdom of Judah and of Israel is only a utopia." See *Actes et Documents du Saint Siège relatifs à la Seconde Guerre Mondiale. No. 9: Le Saint Siège et les Victimes de la Guerre. Janvier-Décembre 1943,* ed. by Pierre Blet, Robert Graham, et al. (Vatican City, 1975), p. 469, doc. 324.

63. *JC*, 23 April 1869, p. 10.

64. Carr, *Spain 1808–1939,* p. 345.

65. Amador, *Historia,* p. 561.

66. *JC*, 29 January 1875, p. 699.

67. *AZJ*, 15 June 1869, p. 476; also 14 September 1869, p. 749.

68. See Carr, *Spain 1808–1939,* pp. 345 and 303.

69. See Menéndez Pelayo, *Historia de los Heterodoxos Españoles* (Madrid, 1880-82), III, 783-98, as quoted by C. J. Bartlett, "The Question of Religious Toleration in Spain in the 19th Century," *Journal of Ecclesiastical History,* 8 (1957), 210.

70. A Madrid correspondent of the *JC*, 2 July 1869, pp. 8-9.

71. *Ibid.*

72. *JC*, 15 January 1864, p. 4.

73. Amador, *Historia,* pp. 562-64.

74. Amador, *Historia,* p. 568. He names sixteen but, curiously, omits to mention the nine "Hebreos" whose names appeared in the official *Gaceta* of 19 August 1871. See *JC*, 22 September 1871, p. 3.

75. *JC*, 9 September 1904, p. 23.

76. See *AZJ*, 13 July 1875, p. 462, quoting *La Correspondencia de España*. According to Léon, *Histoire des Juifs*, p. 357, no one was in fact molested at that time. Referring to the settlement of Jewish businessmen in the 1840s and 1850s, he writes: "Pendant les premières années, où encore aucune loi de tolérance n'avait été édictée, quoiqu'aucun n'eût caché sa religion, personne ne fut ni inquiété ni insulté dans sa liberté de conscience. . . . Quelques négociants plus pieux, lorsqu'ils étaient à St-Sébastien, recevaient même leur viande *cocher*, au su et au vu de tout le monde, et la douane la laissait passer librement."

77. Carr, *Spain 1808–1939*, p. 351.

78. Atkinson, *History of Spain and Portugal*, pp. 299 and 303.

79. *AZJ*, 25 May 1875, p. 351.

80. *Ibid.*, 2 November 1875, p. 730.

81. Carr, *Spain 1808–1939*, p. 351 and note 3.

82. Amador, *Historia*, pp. 565-66.

83. Anglo-Jewish Association, *Fifth Annual Report 1875-76* (London, 1876), pp. 14-17.

84. The proceedings of the Deputies were reported in the *JC*, 14 April 1876, p. 23. See also the letter from the Solicitor to the Board of Deputies by Lewis Emanuel, in *JC*, 16 September 1881, p. 5.

85. 19 April 1876. The article was reprinted in the *JC*, 21 April 1876, p. 37.

86. Baron de las Cuatro Torres; quoted in *AZJ*, 27 June 1876, p. 421.

87. Madrid report of the *Kölnische Zeitung*; quoted in *AZJ*, 30 May 1876, p. 357.

88. Statement in the Cortes on 12 May 1876, quoted by Bartlett, "The Question of Religious Toleration," p. 213.

89. See Lewis Emanuel's Letter in *JC*, 16 September 1881, p. 5. Also, *AZJ*, 16 May 1876, p. 321; 30 May 1876, p. 356; and Carr, *Spain 1808–1939*, p. 352.

90. See *AZJ*, 16 May 1876, p. 321; also *JC*, 16 September 1881, p. 5.

91. See the editorial, "Spain and the Jews," *JC*, 26 May 1876, p. 121.

92. In a letter to Guedalla, dated 27 June 1881; quoted in *JC*, 9 September 1904, p. 23.

93. Atkinson, *History of Spain and Portugal*, p. 304.

94. *JC*, 18 May 1877, p. 12. Assurances to the same effect were repeated in 1881 (Emanuel, *Century and a Half*, p. 114); in a Cortes debate of 12 February 1882 (*AZJ*, 4 April, p. 221); in a statement in the Cortes on 11 February 1887 (Léon, *Histoire des Juifs*, p. 361; and *AZJ*, 10 March 1887, p. 155; also *AZJ*, 19 May 1887, p. 309); and in 1892, the 400th anniversary of the expulsion, cited in Angel Pulido Fernández, *Los Israelitas Españoles y el Idioma Castellano* (Madrid, 1904), pp. 211-12.

95. Royal Order quoted in Pulido, *Los Israelitas Españoles*, p. 209.

96. Simon Dubnow, *History of the Jews in Russia and Poland* (Philadelphia, 1916), I, 131 f., notes that "originally the Jewish physicians of Poland were natives either of Spain whence they had been expelled in 1492, or of Italy . . ." For the details of this episode see Manuel Fernández Rodríguez, "España y los Judíos en el Reinado de Alfonso XII," *Historia*, 25 (1965), 565-84. This essay includes nine archival documents, of which eight were issued by the Spanish Legation in Constantinople (June-September 1881) and one a French document dated 12 July 1882. It was a petition of 58 Jewish families asking permission to settle on agricultural land in Spain.

97. Reuter report in *JC*, 24 June 1881, p. 12.

98. E.g., *El Progreso* quoted in *AZJ*, 19 July 1881, p. 481.

99. Pulido, *Los Israelitas Españoles*, pp. 210-11.

100. E. N. Adler, "Auto da Fé," *The Jewish Quarterly Review* (1901). 392.

101. Editorial, *JC*, 24 June 1881, pp. 11-12.

102. *AZJ*, 16 August 1881, p. 544.

103. Quoted at length in *AZJ*, 19 May 1887, pp. 308-309. See *JC*, 3 June 1887, p. 11. Also,

Raymond Renard, *"Sepharad." Le monde et la langue judéo-espagnole des Sephardim* (Belgium, 1970), p. 194; and Léon, *Histoire des Juifs,* pp. 361-62.

104. *JC,* 8 October 1886, p. 13; 7 April 1876, p. 6; 1 July 1881, p. 4 and 19 July 1884, p. 11.

105. *Jahrbuch für jüdische Geschichte und Literatur* (Berlin, 1900), III, 16. In 1904 a Professor of History at the University of Madrid, Antonio Sanchez Moguel, thought there were "about three hundred [Jewish] families" in Seville, according to Dr. Meyer Kayserling, "Spanien und die Juden," *AZJ,* 23 December 1904, p. 616. Seville was then believed to be the only large city in Spain with any actual Jewish life. See Dr. Abraham Shalom Yahuda, "The Jews in Modern Spain," *JC,* 17 April 1914, p. 17.

106. In San Sebastian some thirty worshipers met for Rosh Hashanah services in 1918 at the villa of M. de Windt. See *JC,* 4 October 1918, p. 10.

107. Pulido, *Españoles sin Patria,* p. 340.

108. See Caro Baroja, *Judíos en la España,* p. 203.

109. See Yahuda, "The Jews in Modern Spain," p. 17.

110. See *JC,* 29 January 1892, p. 14, in its obituary on Baron de Weisweiller who died at the age of 78; also the obituary on Bauer, *ibid.,* 14 June 1895, p. 8.

111. *JC,* 27 November 1868, p. 6. The sum corresponds roughly to 1,600 million silver pesetas.

112. *AZJ,* 1 June 1869, p. 441. Weisweiller was in touch with Sir Moses Montefiore in 1864, and his "high position as a banker and the Consul of more than one foreign power rendered him highly influential even with the Court," according to Lucien Wolf, *Moses Montefiore,* pp. 218-19. (See above Note 54). Earlier Jewish residents are mentioned in a letter from Albert Hyamson in *JC,* 23 June 1899, p. 10.

113. Caro Baroja, *Judíos en la España,* p. 188.

114. They are probably the bankers referred to in *JC,* 20 November 1868, p. 6.

115. *JC,* 1 June 1860, p. 7, remarking that this was done "without enquiry as to his religion."

116. Atkinson, *History of Spain and Portugal,* pp. 287-88. See *AZJ,* 11 May 1869, p. 384. In fact, says Carr, *Spain 1808-1939,* p. 271, "that so much of the energy for expansion had come from Paris meant that Spain was in danger of becoming an economic dependency of France; the Pereire brothers and the Rothschilds looked as if they might accomplish by their capital what Napoleon I had failed to accomplish by his arms." Cf. also, Léon, *Histoire des Juifs,* p. 338.

117. Carr, *Spain 1808-1939,* pp. 265 and 271.

118. *JC,* 7 April 1876, p. 6; 16 November 1877, p. 7; also 5 October 1888, p. 7.

119. Caro Baroja, *Judíos en la España,* p. 192; also Amador, *Historia,* p. 568.

120. Caro Baroja, *ibid.,* pp. 201, 194. Miguel de Unamuno who regarded antisemitism — "a true Germanic product, even in Russia and France" — as "largely hatred of intelligence and internationalism," referred to some "obsessed by the devil" who at that time were "trying to acclimatize antisemitism in Salamanca by translating Drumont." See the letter to Cansinos-Assens dated 10 July 1917, printed in Rafael Cansinos-Assens, *España y los Judíos Españoles* (Tortosa, 1919), p. 117.

121. Caro Baroja, *Judíos en la España,* p. 193. See also Lea, *History of the Inquisition,* (1907), III, 316; he quotes the earlier "pious Franciscan's" book, *Los Judíos en España* (Madrid, 1881), pp. 44 and 48, which he says "declared that bringing [the Jews] was a sin of moral and political treason and that they would devour the whole Spanish nation."

122. Caro Baroja, *Judíos en la España,* pp. 187 and 192.

123. *JC,* 18 July 1884, p. 11.

124. Pulido, *Españoles sin Patria,* pp. 1 and 6.

125. Atkinson, *History of Spain and Portugal,* p. 311. *Ibid.;* also Carr, *Spain 1808-1939,* pp. 473 and 524.

126. Renard, *"Sepharad,"* p. 194.

127. In an article "Spanien und die Juden," in *AZJ*, 23 December 1904, p. 617.

128. *Jahrbuch für jüdische Geschichte und Literatur* (Berlin, 1906), IX, 11-12.

129. Siegwart M. Nussbaum, "Eine Judenfrage in Spanien," *Frankfurter Zeitung*, 1 October 1905, no. 272.

130. Pulido, *Españoles sin Patria*, pp. 181; 191; 356.

131. *JC*, 11 December 1908, p. 14.

132. In an article in *JC*, 21 November 1913, p. 16.

133. *Ibid.*

134. *Jewish Daily Bulletin*, New York, 19 February 1925, p. 3.

135. *Enciclopedia Universal Ilustrada Europeo-Americana* (Madrid-Barcelona-Bilbao, 1922), XLVIII, 482.

136. Caro Baroja, *Judíos en la España*, p. 202. Pulido may have been responsible for such demonstrations of pro-Jewish feeling as occurred in a *Revista Crítica* (founded early in 1908) with which he was associated and in several articles in the daily *El País*—"facts [said the *Revista's* editor, Señora Carmen de Burgos] which, not even many years ago, would have caused great surprise." See *JC*, 8 March 1908, p. 10. Occasionally, Pulido let his enthusiasm get the better of him, such as his assertion in one of his "Sephardic Letters" (in the *Revista*) that, while Spain had received the Jewish refugees from Casablanca in August 1907, Gibraltar was closed to them. Actually, many of them were accommodated in the British colony. See *JC*, 23 August 1907, p. 10, and A. B. M. Serfaty, *The Jews of Gibraltar under British Rule* (Gibraltar, 1958), p. 31.

137. *American Jewish Year Book*, 11 (1909-1910), 137, hereafter quoted as *AJYB*. See also Jesús Cantera Ortiz de Urbina, *Les Sephardim: Thèmes Espagnoles* (Madrid, 1965), no. 352, p. 6.

138. *AJYB*, 15 (1913-1914), 343.

139. Madrid correspondent of the London *Times*, 13 June 1910, p. 7; also *JC*, 17 June 1910, p. 9.

140. *The Times*, 13 June 1910, p. 7.

141. Madrid correspondent of *The Times*, 22 May 1905, p. 5.

142. Letter by the Commissary of the Council of (Anglican) Bishops, Thomas J. Pulvertaft, in *The Times*, 26 May 1905, p. 7. Oddly enough, the king to whom the protest was addressed declared himself in sympathy with the bishop and promised to do what he could to oblige. He probably was a little disingenuous, diplomatically, and the government deprecated the "exaggerated importance" that was being attached to the "old world style of such correspondence customary in Spain" (Madrid report in *The Times*, 22 May 1905, p. 5). Even so, some, like the *Alliance Israélite Universelle*, raised an eyebrow: if this was done to Protestants, what hope was there for Jews? The deduction was not perhaps strictly correct. If only because they did not proselytize, Jews were, on the whole, regarded with less disfavor than Protestants. In a letter to the *Alliance's* magazine *L'Univers Israélite*, Pulido insisted that Spanish liberals would permit no relapse into intolerance but, on the contrary, would press for an ever more broadminded interpretation of the constitution. While some of the clergy were still diehards, he wrote, many bishops and priests were supporting the campaign. See *Der Israelit*, Mayence, 27 July 1905, p. 1297.

143. *Jahrbuch für jüdische Geschichte und Literatur* (Berlin, 1911), XIV, 11.

144. It is perhaps fair to remark in this context that even now synagogues in Spain are not always recognizable as such. Searching for one in Málaga in October 1975, I discovered it near the Palace of Justice in a very modern tall building (Duquesa de Parcent, 3) whose tenants included the British Consulate; but whereas this was clearly marked outside, nothing indicated the presence of a synagogue (and the office of the *Comunidad Israelita*) on the third floor.

145. Yahuda, "The Jews in Modern Spain," p. 17.

146. *JC*, 9 June 1905, p. 25.

147. Editorial, *ibid.*, p. 8.

148. *Ungarische Wochenschrift*, ed. by Julius Gabel, quoted in *Der Israelit*, 20 July 1905, p. 1251 with qualified approval.

149. *The Letters and Papers of Chaim Weizmann* (London, Jerusalem, 1975), Series A. Letters, June 1905–December 1906, IV, 270. At the time of the Algeciras Conference (April 1906), the *Alliance Israélite Universelle* complimented the Spanish foreign minister on the "never to be forgotten words" with which he had supported the suggestions of the United States in favor of Moroccan Jews, "so many of whom [the Duke of Almovodar had said] are attached to Spain by ties of descent and community of language," see *JC*, 13 April 1906, p. 12. A reader's letter in *ibid.*, 20 April 1906, p. 18, "strongly protested against any expressions of gratitude to Spain" whose "attitude towards us was typical of most of our enemies. They are all kind enough to express their horror and indignation at occurrences outside their dominion, but they can never see their way to ameliorate the condition of the Jews in their own countries." Gaster, on the other hand, persisted in his view when he delivered a sermon after an attempt had been made on the life of King Alfonso in 1906: "To our honour as Jews, it must be said that we have never retained a deep-seated grudge against nations and kings who have persecuted us. The desire of vengeance has never taken root in our heart. We have always left it to God to right the wrong—'Mine is the vengeance and I requite,' says the Lord. And we knew that God's justice would sooner or later overtake the evil-doers. Has not Spain been visited by God's requital for the wrong done to the Jews in centuries gone by? Have they not paid, in loss of honour, prosperity and freedom for the misery caused by unbridled fanaticism? And has not every nation and every person that have raised their hands against our people felt the weight of God's punishment for their wicked deeds? If we were to retain the feeling of hatred against those who in ages past have sinned cruelly against us, is there any nation in Europe from which we would not turn in hatred and abhorrence? But happily we Jews know not undying hatred. If anything, we too easily forgive and forget." *Ibid.*, 8 June 1906, p. 28.

150. *JC*, 3 January 1913, p. 17. See also Professor Yahuda in an interview with the *JC*, 9 May 1919, p. 14.

151. *The New York Times*, 5 June 1917, p. 3. King Alfonso himself is believed to have shown a direct interest in the matter. In the course of an audience, reported in *JC*, 7 May 1920, p. 16, Prof. Yahuda thanked the king on behalf of Jewish communities in America, Argentina, Britain, Holland, Italy and Egypt. See also Yahuda's article in the *Jewish Forum*, (April 1941), 51–53, entitled, "King Alfonso XIII and the Jews: His action in saving Palestine Jewry from wholesale evacuation."

152. *JC*, 10 June 1910, p. 10. Also *JC*, 17 June 1910, p. 6.

153. *JC*, 18 June 1909, p. 10; also Caro Baroja, *Judíos en la España*, p. 229.

154. In an interview with *Le Matin*, Paris, reported in *JC*, 10 January 1913, p. 16.

155. See Dr. Max Nordau, "Dr. Yahuda's Triumph," *JC*, 7 January 1916, p. 12.

156. *JC*, 21 November 1913, p. 16.

157. *JC*, 24 October 1913, p. 12.

158. Obituary on Pulido in *JC*, 16 December 1932, p. 14.

159. *JC*, 9 May 1919, p. 14.

160. "Kayserling," *Encyclopaedia Judaica* (1971), X., 856.

161. Caro Baroja, *Judíos en la España*, p. 204.

162. *JC*, 9 May 1919, p. 14.

163. For all the details, see Dr. Max Nordau, "Dr. Yahuda and the Madrid University," *JC*, 9 April 1920, pp. 6 and 12–13.

164. Anna and Maxa Nordau, *Max Nordau: A Biography* (New York, 1943), pp. 222; 221; 245.

165. *Ibid.*, 241–242.

166. *JC*, 9 May 1919, p. 14.

167. Nordau, *Nordau: Biography,* p. 242.

168. *JC*, 16 December 1932, p. 14.

169. Nordau, *Nordau: Biography,* p. 242.

170. *JC*, 2 March 1917, p. 10.

171. Nordau, *Nordau: Biography,* p. 243.

172. Renard, *"Sepharad."* p. 195.

173. *JC*, 2 March 1917, p. 10.

174. Cansinos-Assens, *España,* p. 91; see also p. 161.

175. Nordau, *Nordau: Biography,* p. 242. Also see Cansinos-Assens, *España,* p. 68–69.

176. Cansinos-Assens, *España,* pp. 73; 20; 22 and 24.

177. Chaim Weizmann, *Trial and Error* (London, 1949), p. 363.

178. Letter dated 15 December 1924, addressed to the *Jewish Daily Bulletin* New York, which published it on 26 December 1924, p. 3, hereafter quoted as *JDB.*

179. *Ibid.*

180. *JC*, 13 June 1924, p. 18.

181. *La Gaceta de Madrid,* 21 December 1924. Also Haim Avni, "Spanish Nationals in Greece and their Fate during the Holocaust," *Yad Vashem Studies on the European Jewish Catastrophe and Resistance* (Jerusalem, 1970), VIII, 37.

182. *Actas del Primer Simposio de Estudios Sefardíes.* Primero de los Actos celebrados con motivo del XXV Anniversario de la Fundación del Consejo Superior de Investigaciones Científicas, Madrid, 1-6 de junio 1964. Ed. by Iacob M. Hassán. (Madrid, 1970), pp. 583-85. Hereafter quoted as *Actas.*

183. *Ibid.*

184. *Ibid.*

185. *AJYB*, 27 (1925–1926), 77.

186. José María Estrugo, "New Spain and the Sephardic Jews," *Jewish Guardian,* London, 28 August 1925, p. 11, hereafter quoted as *JG.* Estrugo wrote a book entitled *El Retorno a Sefard: Un siglo después de la inquisición* (Madrid, 1933). According to Caro Baroja, *Judíos en la España,* p. 210, "the book was read and discussed by some journalists and men of letters but its influence did not go further."

187. Spanish government memorandum accompanying the decree of 29 December 1948, summarized in *The Wiener Library Bulletin,* 3 (September-November 1949), 39.

188. Estrugo, *El Retorno,* pp. 30-31.

189. Interview with *Revista de la Raza,* Madrid, quoted in *JDB,* 26 February 1925, p. 2.

190. Henry V. Besso, "Decadencia del Judeo-Español. Perspectivas para el Futuro," *Actas,* p. 255.

191. *JDB,* 12 December 1924, p. 3; also *JC,* 5 December 1924, p. 21.

192. *JDB,* 19 July 1927, p. 4.

193. Besso, "Decadencia," p. 255. An instructive article on the Institute "Arias Montano" appeared in the Madrid monthly *España Hoy: Revista de Actualidad Permanente,* 7 (1970), 17-20; "Altas instituciones culturales: El Instituto de Estudios Hebraicos 'Arias Montano' del Consejo Superior de Investigaciones Científicas. La Cultura Sefardí."

194. Jewish Telegraphic Agency report from Shanghai in *JDB,* 30 April 1925, p. 1.

195. *Actas,* p. 582, Appendix 4: "Nota sobre concesión de nacionalidad española a los judíos Sefarditas."

196. Estrugo, "New Spain," *JG,* p. 11.

197. See *AJYB*, 33 (1931-1932) 74.

198. Statement made when he received the Chief Rabbi of Sweden, Dr. Marcus Ehrenpreis, cited in *JC*, 29 July 1927, p. 40.

199. *JC*, 5 February 1926, p. 21.

200. Pulido in *JDB*. (See Note 178).

201. See *JDB*, 30 October 1924, p. 3, where Bauer-Landauer writes on "Hispanic-Jewish Rapprochement;" also *JG*, 20 February 1924, p. 4, where it is curiously, inaccurately, stated that "his parents and brothers all became Catholics."

202. The books were: *Figuras Ibéricas. El Doctor Pulido* (Madrid, 1922); and *Los Hebreos en Marruecos* (Madrid, 1934). See Caro Baroja, *Judíos en la España*, p. 206.

203. *AJYB*, 21 (1919-1920) 299.

204. Victor Salmador, *Don Juan de Borbón. Grandeza y servidumbre del deber* (Madrid, 1976). Extract printed in *ABC*, 21 April 1976, p. 13.

205. Africano Fernández, *España en Africa y el peligro judío. Apuntes de un testigo desde 1915 a 1918:* Caro Baroja, *Judíos en la España*, p. 205.

206. Caro Baroja, *ibid.* 208. The nephew innocently remarks that some of Pio's best friends were Jews. See also p. 206.

207. An American rabbi, Leon H. Elmaleh of Philadelphia, then traveling in Spain found the people "gentle, kindly, courteous, good-tempered, but proud and hot-headed, ignorant, abysmally ignorant and illiterate, and we all know that ignorance breeds savagery and hate"; here was (he went on) "the most inflammable material for any interest desiring to foment race-prejudice and hatred, and could we put our trust in the enlightened and educated classes today?" Cited in *JC*, 24 April 1931, Literary Supplement, III, "Judeo-Spanish Landmarks."

208. Carr, *Spain 1808-1939*, p. 601.

209. Editorial, *JC*, 24 April 1931, p. 6.

210. See *JC*, 24 April 1931, p. 12, an interview with Professor Yahuda: "King Alfonso and the Jews." Also Yahuda's article, "King Alfonso XIII," *Jewish Forum*, 51-53.

211. *JG*, 3 July 1931, p. 3.

212. *JG*, 15 May 1931, p. 3.

213. *JG*, 29 May 1931, p. 3.

214. *JDB*, 24 February 1925, p. 2.

215. *JG*, 29 May 1931, p. 3.

216. *AJYB*, 33 (1931-1932) 73.

217. *AJYB*, 34 (1932-1933), 61. Also Yahuda, "King Alfonso," *JC*. See Note 210.

218. Text in *Actas*, pp. 590-92.

219. *AJYB*, 34 (1932-1933), 61.

220. Carr, *Spain 1808-1939*, pp. 606-607.

221. *AJYB*, 34 (1932-1933) 61.

222. Carr, *Spain 1808-1939*, p. 312.

223. *JC*, 24 April 1931, p. 6.

224. *JC*, 7 December 1934, p. 25.

225. *JC*, 4 January 1935, p. 23.

226. *JG*, 3 July 1931, p. 3.

227. *AJYB*, 33 (1931-1932), 74, erroneously describes it as "the first synagogue since the expulsion."

228. See *JG*, 26 June 1931, p. 5, reporting a marriage of "the first professors of the Jewish religion in Spain since 1492." Rabbi Coriat, officiating, was said to be "now in Madrid representing the Jewish community to get the new Republic which has already decreed liberty of conscience, to repeal the edict of expulsion." After a visit to the synagogue in 1933, Rabbi Baruch Braunstein, counsellor to Jewish students at Columbia University, New York, wrote: "The glory of Spanish Judaism reduced to this hovel! How are the mighty fallen: from Toledo and Granada and Córdoba to this miserable, furtive Synagogue with a poverty-stricken handful of Jews from all over the world." "In Spain Today," *JC*, 20 October 1933, p. 26.

229. Its reestablishment was reported to have been due to the goodwill of a friend of the

king whose daughter was a lady-in-waiting to the queen. If this was so, the *JC*, 9 January 1931, p. 9, remarked, the "recrudescence of Judaism in Spain" was "going on the old undesirable way of Court favouritism." The synagogue apparently ceased to function soon since the very knowledgeable special correspondent of the *JC* in 1934 (Israel Cohen?) does not even mention it.

230. *JC*, 9 January 1931, p. 9; 15 May 1931, p. 19; 5 June 1931, p. 23; 3 July 1931, p. 3.

231. He was said to have publicly declared pride in his Marrano descent: *JC*, 25 December 1931, pp. 5-6.

232. *JC*, 8 January 1932, p. 17.

233. *JC*, 22 January 1932, p. 20.

234. Estrugo, *El Retorno,* pp. 125-30. He also quotes, on pp. 129-31, a supporting press comment from *El Liberal,* Madrid, 22 December 1932.

235. *AJYB*, 38 (1936-1937), 272, mentions 144 naturalized on 5 June 1936.

236. *Actas,* p. 582.

237. Estrugo, *El Retorno,* pp. 121-23.

238. *JC*, 29 March 1935, p. 32.

239. Caro Baroja, *Judíos en la España,* p. 209, n. 35.

240. *JC*, 5 April 1935, p. 26.

241. Arieh Tartakower and Kurt R. Grossmann, *The Jewish Refugee,* (New York, 1944), p. 313. According to official figures quoted in *JC*, 4 January 1935, p. 23, the number of Germans who settled there since 1 March 1933, was 3,000, the great majority Jews. Some opened a then new, one-price store (called SEPU) in Madrid; it proved very popular despite an attempt by a bishop to engineer a boycott of it. See *JC*, 7 December 1934, p. 25.

242. Norman Bentwich, *The Refugees from Germany, 1933-1935* (London, 1936), p. 63.

243. Relating this in his book *Spain* (London, 1942), pp. 363-64, Madariaga states he himself demurred on the ground that "Spain owed it to the millions of Spanish Jews scattered all over the world . . . to take a share in this work of world-statesmanship." If the minister, a "distinguished medievalist," held "unenlightened views," Madariaga added, it was to be remembered that he had been "elected for a province of deep religious and clerical prejudices, Avila." (Yet another such constituency, La Coruña, elected the Jew, Gustave Bauer, in 1910: *ibid.*, note 152.)

244. The petition by Franz Bernheim, a Jewish resident of Gleiwitz, Upper Silesia, claimed that Germany had violated the German-Polish convention on Upper Silesia, of 15 May 1922, in respect to the pledges given by her for the equal rights of persons belonging to racial, religious and linguistic minorities, which had been placed under the guarantee of the League of Nations. For the full text of the Bernheim Petition see *AJYB*, 35 (1933-1934), 74-78.

245. Speech in the Council of the League of Nations on 30 May 1933: *AJYB*, 35 (1933-1934), 86; 87.

246. *AJYB*, 36 (1934-1935) 97.

247. *Unity in Dispersion. A History of the World Jewish Congress* (New York, 1948), p. 114. Also *JC*, 22 January 1937, p. 20.

248. Statement made to Rabbi Baruch Braunstein who reported it in *JC*, 20 October 1933, p. 26.

249. Nor could it withstand the tide of events. After first refusing a government subsidy to the Spanish team for the International Olympic Games held in Berlin, Prime Minister Manuel Azaña explained that, though he personally was opposed to Spain's participation, the government was obliged to follow the example of other democratic states. See *JC*, 28 February 1936, p. 17, and *AJYB*, 38 (1936-1937), 271-72.

250. See *JC*, 4 January 1935, p. 23; also Rabbi Baruch Braunstein: "Those thought patterns into which the Church moulded Spain in the sixteenth century are still the thought patterns of the overwhelming number of Spaniards. . . . To the mind of Spain the Jew is still the devil and the heretic outcast." See *JC*, 20 October 1933, p. 26.

251. See *The Times,* London, 13 June 1910, p. 7.

252. Richard A. H. Robinson, *The Origins of Franco's Spain. The Right, the Republic and Revolution 1931–36* (Pittsburgh, Pa., 1970), p. 69. Also Caro Baroja, *Judíos en la España*, p. 210, quotes a booklet "representative" of this propaganda: *Los poderes ocultos en España. Los Protocolos y su aplicación a España. Infiltraciones masónicas en el Catolicismo* (Barcelona, 1932).

253. Carr, *Spain 1808–1939*, p. 607.

254. Caro Baroja, *Judíos en la España*, p. 211.

255. Lucien Wolf's pamphlet on *The Jewish Bogey* (London, 1920) was translated by Jehuda Sefardí under the title *El fantasma judío y los falsos protocolos de los ancianos sabios de Sión* (1933). For the unfolding crime, see S. Valentí Camp y S. Velasco, *La odisea de los judíos, El trágico sino de una raza* (Barcelona, 1933).

256. *JC*, 22 January 1932, p. 20.

257. *JC*, 7 December 1934, p. 25.

258. Carr, *Spain 1808–1939*, p. 608.

259. *AJYB*, 38 (1936–1937), 271.

260. *JC*, 7 December 1934, p. 25.

261. *Mi lucha.* (Barcelona, Casa Editorial Araluce).

262. Caesar Caspar, "Mein Kampf—A Best Seller," *Jewish Social Studies*, 20 (January 1958), 14.

263. *JC*, 30 April 1937, p. 34, Also, *JC*, 19 February 1937, p. 20: letter by L. de Armas, writing from nationalist headquarters at Salamanca.

264. "Which was at once Franco's quick weekly guide to events and the ruling party's guide to thought and action," according to Brian Crozier, *Franco. A Biographical History* (London, 1967), p. 268.

265. Crozier, *ibid.* About the same time, the Franco authorities published an anthology of Pio Baroja's antisemitic writings! (Caro Baroja, *Judíos en la España*, p. 208).

266. Crozier, *ibid.*

267. *Völkischer Beobachter*, 30 August 1936, quoted in Louis W. Bondy, *Racketeeers of Hatred. Julius Streicher and the Jew-baiters' International* (London, 1946), p. 210.

268. *JC*, 7 August 1936, p. 16.

269. In its issue of 2 February 1937, for example, *Arriba* reprinted cartoons from the *Stürmer's* Special Edition, 5 (September 1936). See Bondy, *Racketeers*, pp. 209–10.

270. *JC*, 19 March 1937, p. 39.

271. *JC*, 30 September 1938, p. 24, in a report headed, "Is Franco Anti-Jewish?"

272. Caro Baroja, *Judíos en la España*, p. 212.

273. Crozier, *Franco*, p. 196.

274. *JC*, 20 May 1938, p. 36, quoting the Republican government's official news agency in Barcelona.

275. *JC*, 24 June 1938, p. 35.

276. Bondy, *Racketeers*, p. 211.

277. *Fränkische Tageszeitung*, Nuremberg, 22 January 1938, quoted by Bondy, *Racketeers*, p. 210.

278. See Crozier, *Franco*, p. 187 for a "long and extraordinary series of broadcasts for which his individual flavouring of venom, oaths, insults and mordant humour always guaranteed an audience."

279. *JC*, 30 April 1937, p. 24.

280. Speech delivered on 12 September 1937, quoted in *AJYB*, 40 (1938–1939), 187.

281. *JC*, 24 September 1937, p. 24.

282. *AJYB*, 40 (1938–1939), 188.

283. *JC*, 17 December 1937, p. 29.

284. *AJYB*, 39 (1937-1938), 324; also *JC*, 21 August 1936, p. 24.

285. *Der Angriff*, Berlin, 30 August 1936, quoted by Bondy, *Racketeers*, p. 210.

286. *JC*, 10 September 1937, p. 17, and 24 June 1938, p. 35.

287. *JC*, 26 February 1937, p. 35; and 26 March 1937, p. 21.

288. *JC*, 26 February 1937, p. 35, quoting a report in the Roman paper, *Giornale d'Italia*.

289. Bondy, *Racketeers*, p. 210, quoting *Der Angriff*.

290. *JC*, 11 February 1938, p. 20.

291. Carr, *Spain 1808-1939*, p. 605.

292. *JC*, 4 September 1936, p. 27, though according to *JC*, 5 August 1938, p. 25, three to four thousand still remained.

293. *JC*, 22 October 1937, p. 31; 2 September 1938, p. 26; 21 June 1940, p. 10; and 22 October 1937, p. 31.

294. *JC*, 30 April 1937, p. 24. A plea to admit Rumanian Sephardim wishing to settle in Spain was made by the Barcelona Labor ("anarchist") daily, *Solidaridad Obrera*, when it attacked the "medieval barbarism" of the Goga regime early in 1938. See *JC*, 11 February 1938, p. 20.

295. *JC*, 22 October 1937, p. 31.

296. *JC*, 14 April 1939, p. 23; 30 April 1937, p. 24.

297. *AJYB*, 42 (1940-1941), 435.

298. *JC*, 26 April 1940, p. 12.

299. In 1940, a number of Greek Jewish families who had left Spain during the Civil War received permission to return and resume their occupations: *JC*, 12 April 1940, p. 22. In Tetuan the authorities were found to be tolerant toward the local Jews, respecting their religious beliefs: *JC*, 3 March 1939, p. 29.

300. *JC*, 4 October 1940, p. 7.

301. Alan Bullock, *Hitler. A Study in Tyranny* (London, 1952), pp. 555-56.

302. Henry Picker, *Hitlers Tischgespräche im Führer-Hauptquartier* (Stuttgart, 1976), p. 427; also see p. 429.

303. Bullock, *Hitler*, 555-56. On this point Dr. Joseph Goebbels, the minister of propaganda, (for once) agreed with Ribbentrop, describing Franco as "either overbearing or craven and cowardly." *Joseph Goebbels. Tagebücher 1945. Die Letzten Aufzeichnungen* (Hamburg, 1977), p. 77.

304. *The Daily Telegraph*, 21 November 1975, p. 6: obituary on Franco.

305. Haim Avni, "La Salvación de Judíos por España durante la Segunda Guerra Mundial," *Actas*, p. 84.

306. *AJYB*, 43 (1941-1942), 201-202.

307. Avni, "La Salvación," p. 82.

308. Malcolm J. Proudfoot, *European Refugees 1939-1952* (London, 1957), pp. 56-57.

309. *AJYB*, 43 (1941-1942), 327-28.

310. Tartakower and Grossmann, *Jewish Refugee*, pp. 313-14.

311. *AJYB*, 43 (1941-1942), 202.

312. Avni, "La Salvación," p. 84.

313. *AJYB*, 44 (1942-1943), 231.

314. *AJYB*, 45 (1943-1944), 294; 295.

315. *AJYB*, 46 (1944-1945), 237.

316. *AJYB*, 45 (1943-1944), 295.

317. *AJYB*, 46 (1944-1945), 237-38.

318. Avni, "La Salvación," pp. 84-86.

319. Caro Baroja, *Judíos en la España*, p. 212. On p. 213, he mentions exceptions

in Bayonne, too. See also, Avni, "La Salvación," p. 86 and Caro Baroja, *Judíos en la España*, p. 213.

320. Caro Baroja, *ibid.*; Avni, *ibid.*, pp. 86–87.

321. Avni, *ibid.*

322. Raul Hilberg, *The Destruction of the European Jews* (London, 1961), pp. 447–48. The first secretary of the Spanish Embassy in Berlin, Señor Diaz-Isasi, told the head of "Inland II" section in the Foreign Office, Eberhard von Thadden (who made a note of it on 21 July 1943), that while willing to agree to a removal of Spanish Jews from Salonika, Spain would not allow "Spanish citizens to be liquidated in Polish camps," *The Wiener Library Bulletin*, 13 (1959), 37.

323. Avni, "La Salvación," p. 88. According to Gerald Reitlinger, *The Final Solution. The Attempt to Exterminate the Jews of Europe* (London, 1953), p. 377, the number was 367.

324. Hilberg, *Destruction*, p. 448.

325. Reitlinger, *Final Solution*, p. 377.

326. Caro Baroja, *Judíos en la España*, p. 213.

327. Avni, "La Salvación," pp. 88–89.

328. *Resolutions. War Emergency Conference of the World Jewish Congress.* Atlantic City, New Jersey, 26–30 November 1944. (New York, n.d.), p. 15.

329. Reported in the Istanbul Ladino paper *La Boz de Türkiye*, 1 March 1948 and reprinted in *Sefarad*, 8 (1948), 239, fasc. 1.

330. Avni, "Spanish Nationals," *Yad Vashem Studies*, p. 67.

331. *AJYB*, 48 (1946–1947), 301.

332. *AJYB*, 46 (1944–1945), 237.

333. Avni, "La Salvación," p. 83, quoting a German Embassy dispatch from Madrid dated 7 November 1941.

334. *Arriba*, Madrid, 14 June 1942, quoted in *Jewish News*, London, 30 June 1942, p. 51.

335. Bondy, *Racketeers*, p. 211.

336. *Historia de los Judíos desde la destrucción del Templo* (Madrid, 1944).

337. See this author's (unsigned) review in *Jewish News*, London, 17 October 1944, p. 249.

338. *Sefarad*, 4 (1944), 416–17, fasc. 2.

339. *Sefarad*, 1 (1941), fasc. 1.

340. See *Actas*, pp. 592–94; also p. 582.

341. *Sefarad*, 9 (1949), 259, fasc. 1.

342. English summary in *The Wiener Library Bulletin*, 3 (1949), 39.

343. "Franco as 'Friend' of the Jews: Motives behind the dictator's New Policy," *Congress Weekly*, New York, 14 February 1949, pp. 5–7.

344. *The New York Times*, 2 October 1948, quoted in *JC*, 8 October 1948, p. 1.

345. *JC*, 15 October 1948, p. 9.

346. See Harry C. Schnur, "In Spain: Invisible Jews," *Congress Weekly*, New York, 12 October 1953, 11–12. Also Caro Baroja, *Judíos en la España*, p. 214.

347. Renard, "*Sepharad*.", p. 196, n. 2.

348. Interview with the *New York Herald Tribune*, quoted in *JC*, 28 January 1949, p. 9.

349. *JC*, 4 February 1949, p. 12, editorial.

350. George Hills, *Franco. The Man and his Nation* (London, 1967), p. 407.

351. *AJYB*, 51 (1950), 388.

352. Hills, *Franco. The Man*, p. 407.

353. Speech delivered on 7 October 1952 and printed in *Comunidades Judías de Latino-américa, 1971-72*. Oficina sudamericana del Comité Judío Americano. Instituto de Relaciones Humanas (Buenos Aires, 1974), pp. 245–50.

354. See the controversy between the Falange paper *Arriba* and the Archbishop of Seville, Cardinal Segura: *New York Herald Tribune*, Paris edition, messages from Seville and Madrid, 11 and 14 March 1952; also 3 May 1952.

355. *Church Times*, London, 30 June 1950, p. 487.

356. Renard,*"Sepharad. "*, p. 196.

357. Interview with Daniel Lawrence, publisher of *US News & World Report*, quoted by the Washington correspondent of the *JC*, 27 May 1955, p. 32.

358. *JC*, 1 January 1960, p. 12.

359. Renard, *"Sepharad."*, p. 197.

360. See Córdoba's daily paper *Córdoba*, 9 June 1964, quoted in *Actas*, p. 635.

361. Madrid correspondent of *The Times*, 13 March 1962, p. 10.

362. Madrid correspondent of the *Frankfurter Rundschau*, 31 March 1962.

363. *New York Herald Tribune*, Paris edition, 28 February 1967, p. 2.

364. Madrid correspondent of *The Times*, 2 March 1967, p. 6.

365. *The New York Times*, 20 January 1967, p. 11.

366. *Amistad Judéo-Cristiana*, Madrid (January-March 1973), 8.

367. "Christian Comment," *Jerusalem Post*, 14 January 1977.

368. Statement published in the journal *Iglesia en Madrid* and quoted in *The Tablet*, London, 22 January 1977, p. 91.

369. Jerry Goodman, "Spain," in *AJYB*, 68 (1967), 337-38.

370. *JC*, 19 March 1965, p. 1.

371. Goodman, "Spain," p. 338.

372. Abraham S. Karlikow, "Spain," in *AJYB*, 74 (1973), 426-27.

373. In an interview with the Madrid daily *El Pueblo*, 13 January 1968.

374. For all details, see *Hakesher*, monthly magazine of the Spanish Jewish communities, Madrid, 39 (January 1969). On 14 December 1968, the minister of justice issued a statement (of which a photocopy is in the author's possession) according legal recognition to "the non-Catholic religious association," *Comunidad Israelita de Madrid*, in response to a petition by its lawfully appointed representatives, Max Mazin Brodowka, Vico Pelosof Arditi and Moisés Bertafy Rofé—"having satisfied himself [the minister writes] that the abrogation of the Royal Decree of 31 March 1492 by the constitution of 5 June 1869 and subsequent legislation has permitted the establishment in Spain of Hebrew congregations which in fact have been in existence for several generations" (*siendo cierto que la derogación de la Real Cédula de 31 de marzo de 1.492 por la Constitución de 5 de junio de 1.869 y la legislación posterior ha permitido el establecimiento en España de comunidades hebreas, que de hecho existen desde hace varias generaciones*).

375. Antonio Aradillas, "Una Sinagoga Española," *El Pueblo*, 17 December 1968.

376. Luis Ulloa Cisneros, "Los Reyes Católicos y la Unidad Nacional," in *Historia de España*, ed. by Luis Dericot Garcia (Barcelona, 1935), III, 411 ff.

377. Andrés Giménez Soler, *Fernando el Católico* (Barcelona, Madrid, 1941), pp. 100-104.

378. César Silió Cortés, *Isabel la Católica, Fundadora de España. Su Vida, su Tiempo, su Reinado, 1451-1504* (Madrid, 1943), p. 311. He also mentions, however, the opinion expressed by Zurano Muñoz, in a book, *Valor y fuerza de España* (Madrid, 1922), that but for the expulsion, Spain "would have won the economic hegemony of the world."

379. Feliciano Cereceda, SJ, *Semblanza Espiritual de Isabel la Católica* (Madrid, 1946), pp. 239-40.

380. R. P. Luis Fernández de Retana, *Isabel la Católica. Fundadora de la Unidad Nacional Española* (Madrid, 1947), II, 51, 55, 61.

381. Ernesto Jiménez Navarro, *La Historia de España* (Madrid, n.d., apparently after 1945), p. 257. Cf. also Juan de Contreras, *Los Orígines del Imperio: La España de Fernando e Isabel* (Madrid, 1966), pp. 78 and 83, who rejoices in the expulsion as an act "to the greater glory of the church."

382. Manuel Ballesteros Gaibrois, *La Obra de Isabel la Católica* (Segovia, 1953), pp. 468 ff.

383. Similar charges are brought by F. Soldevila, *Historia de España* (Barcelona, 1954), III, 169.

384. Luis de Armiñan, *Isabel la Reina Católica* (Madrid, 1951), pp. 313 ff.

385. *JC*, 29 August 1969, p. 16.

386. A plaque at the entrance to the synagogue reads: "El Rey Alfonso XIII ordenó la Consolidación y Conservación de este Monumento." See Yahuda, "King Alfonso XIII," *Jewish Forum*, 53.

387. *JC*, 18 June 1971, p. 4.

388. See *Arriba*, 29 May 1976, p. 8; *Ya*, 29 May 1976, p. 2; also *JC*, 4 June 1976, p. 1.

389. *Jerusalem Post*, 9–10 December 1976.

390. *International Herald Tribune*, Paris, 30 November 1976.

391. *News & Views from the Secretary General of the World Jewish Congress*, Geneva, 1, 3 (January 1977) 2.

392. A report in the *JC*, 10 December 1976, p. 1, said: "Jewry figuratively stood this week by the graveside of Torquemada. . . . It was a living demonstration of victory over the enemies of Jews, from Pharaoh to Hitler, via Haman and the Spanish Inquisition."

393. *JC*, 3 December 1976, p. 1.

394. There is no evidence to support the capricious assertion: see Note 1.

395. See the reports in *El País*, *El Pueblo* and *Informaciones*, Madrid, all 4 December 1976.

396. *The New York Times*, 6 December 1976, p. 18.

397. *Arriba*, 4 December 1976.

398. *Diario 16*, quoted in *The Christian Science Monitor*, 6 December 1976.

399. *JC*, 10 December 1976, p. 40.

400. *The New York Times*, 7 December 1976, p. 2.

401. *Ya*, 5 December 1976. See also, *JC*, 30 December 1977, p. 28.

402. *El Pueblo*, 7 December 1976.

403. *Jerusalem Post*, 6 December 1976.

404. *El País*, 4 December 1976.

405. Madrid correspondent of *The Times*, 6 December 1976, p. 4.

406. Statement by Yitzhak Navon, speaker of the Knesset, reported in the Jewish Telegraphic Agency's *Daily News Bulletin*, London, 9 December 1976, p. 1, hereafter called *JTA*.

407. Yigal Allon, Israeli Foreign Minister: *JTA*, 9 December 1976, p. 4. Also *The New York Times*, 9 December 1976, p. 6.

408. Navon, *JTA*, p. 1.

409. Quoted in *Jerusalem Post*, 7–8 December 1976.

410. *JTA*, 10 December 1976, p. 1.

411. *JC*, 17 December 1976, p. 19.

412. *International Herald Tribune*, 30 November 1976.

413. *Jerusalem Post*, 28 March 1977.

414. *Frankfurter Allgemeine Zeitung*, 11 January 1977.

415. *El País*, the liberal daily, quoted in *International Herald Tribune*, 30 November 1976.

416. *JTA*, 1 March 1977, p. 2.

INDEX OF NAMES

3 5282 00061 2930